The world has cha

Teenagers exist in a different world than you grew up in. Video games, gun violence, sexting, and bullying have all exploded onto the scene, leaving many parents shut off from their children and vice versa. In that vacuum, too many kids gravitate toward darker temptations, but there is hope.

You are not alone.

Come behind the scenes and walk the halls with school resource officer Jack Hobson, Ed.D. Firsthand, he witnessed the scenarios that caused good students to turn bad or troubled teens to clean up their act. Sometimes, the difference could be a few simple words from the right person to stop the dangerous drift toward delinquency or worse.

Some students drifted back. Others did not. These are their stories.

KUDOS for *Drifters*

In *Drifters: Stories from the Dark Side of Delinquency*, Dr. Jack Hobson gives us an intriguing look at high schools today and what really constitutes school security. The book has tons of good information in it for those of us who have to deal with teens on a regular basis and spend most of our time scratching our heads over the things they do. *Drifters* is timely, thought-provoking, and informative. It is also very entertaining. – *Taylor Jones, reviewer*

Drifters: Stories from the Dark Side of Delinquency by Jack Hobson, Ed.D. is a fascinating read. The book is overflowing with useful information on dealing with teenagers, as well as giving us a glimpse into what these kids go through during their high school years. I found myself caught up in their stories, rooting for kids I've never met. I thought *Drifters* was insightful, well-written, and a pleasure to read. – *Regan Murphy, reviewer*

A sometimes funny, sometimes heartbreaking book that reads like a novel. Dr. Hobson illuminates what really goes on within our schools today. Even better, he offers hope. – *Bonnie Hearn Hill, best-selling author*

Drifters is an eye-opening journey behind the curtains of high school delinquency. This book is as captivating as it is relevant. Jack Hobson takes advantage of his unique position to tell the tales of the dark side of our country's educational system, so that hopefully we won't continue to make the same mistakes with the students who need our help the most. – *Christopher Allan Poe, author of* The Portal.

DRIFTERS

Stories from the Dark Side
of Delinquency

by

Jack Hobson, Ed.D.

A BLACK OPAL BOOKS PUBLICATION

GENRE: NON-FICTION/SELF-HELP/PSYCHOLOGY

This book is a work of non-fiction. All information and opinions expressed herein are the views of the author. This publication is intended to provide accurate and authoritative information concerning the subject matter covered and is for informational purposes only. Neither the author nor the publisher is attempting to provide medical or legal advice of any kind.

DRIFTERS: Stories from the Dark Side of Delinquency
Copyright © 2013 by Jack Hobson, Ed.D.
Cover Design by Christopher Allan Poe
All cover art copyright © 2013
All Rights Reserved
Print ISBN: 978-1-62694081-9

First Publication: NOVEMBER 2013

Published by Black Opal Books: http://www.blackopalbooks.com

DEDICATION

For Nancy, Mo grai, Mo saoil

TABLE of CONTENTS

FOREWORD

By

Carolyn Petrosino, Ph.D., Professor, Criminal Justice, Bridgewater State University, Bridgewater, Massachusetts, June 2013, co-author of *American Corrections – The Brief*, Cengage

I fell in love with the field of criminal justice shortly after discovering it. Today I am enjoying a career that now spans more than 30 years. I've had a variety of powerful experiences, including working with at-risk kids in a community setting and assisting the efforts of incarcerated offenders who made attempts at rehabilitation. I also worked as a Hearing Officer for the New Jersey State Parole Board for more than 10 years. For the past 20 years, I've been in academia, teaching a variety of courses.

It is this background that allows me to fully appreciate the work of Jack Hobson and his book, *Drifters*. You see, our paths are similar. His experience as a practitioner also superseded his own voyage into academia. Jack first worked as a police officer coming face to face with those who had entered the world of crime; he then became a School Resource Officer (SRO), engaging with students on the cusp of delinquency and criminality.

I came to know Jack after he moved into academia, while I was Criminal Justice Department Chairperson at Bridgewater State University. Appreciating his experience in law enforcement and his reflective insights as an instructor, I did a very smart thing and recruited him to become a Visiting Professor for our department. He has been an invaluable colleague and instructor ever since.

Jack is the complete package in my view. He possesses both street and book knowledge. He knows how to make the best use of both. He is also a caring and compassionate person about many things, and his life's work has been about helping young people, improving the criminal justice system, enforcing ethical principles in police work, establishing fairness, and emphasizing the respect and dignity of others.

Due to his professional experiences and unique perspective, readers of *Drifters* can be assured that this book is written by someone who understands the integrated world of public schools, troubled youth, the reach of the juvenile justice system, and the potential of the School Resource Officer.

With increased concern about school violence, School Resource Officers (SRO) have become more commonplace in the public school system. Quelling violence in our schools is a high priority. With the mass shooting at the Sandy Hook Elementary School, in Newtown, Connecticut, fresh in our minds, we all wish to see the threat of violence in our schools reduced to zero. But more common than mass shootings, are young people walking precariously on the edge of delinquency, criminality and yes, violence. As a SRO, Jack Hobson saw his role as going beyond crisis management and providing security. It was also about delinquency and crime prevention. He took on the challenge of changing an ominous trajectory of some students before they are catapulted into the juvenile or adult criminal justice system. He took on the challenge of confronting *drift*.

This is a unique and important book. Not because it announces the next hopeful crime theory or program that promises to rid our society of the evils of juvenile delinquency. No. The contribution of this book is that it is revelatory. It makes explicit the ever-changing mindset of teenagers and it takes the concept of *drift* and animates it through the lives of the young people who came across Hobson's path as an SRO. Drift theory contends that juveniles who hold to conventional values, ideals and practices will periodically engage in delinquent behavior that runs counter to these values. They justify their law violating (or delinquent) behavior with specific arguments or neutralizations that allow them to suspend pro-social values and legitimize delinquent behavior. Hobson puts a face and personality on kids that drift as he describes his various encounters.

The subjects of Hobson's book are those kids living out a *drift* period in their lives. They were not raised in *Leave it to Beaver* households, but neither were their homes totally dysfunctional. Likewise, his subjects are not perfect kids, but neither do they have one-way tickets to state prison. They are, however, in states of drift.

As a SRO, Jack did more than merely go on auto pilot and apply the letter of the law to students for their missteps. His book describes his efforts to yank some of these students out of drift and into a place where they became more positive about themselves, and in which they began setting goals and meeting expectations (even if they were small ones).

This book will leave the reader with a true sense of hope. Today's youth are living in a far different world than previous generations. Their world goes at a much faster pace, risk taking is not viewed by them as risky at all, and younger and younger students are engaged with issues and problems that, many years ago, were dealt with only by adults.

Too often some youth feel increasingly isolated even in the age of Facebook, Twitter and other social media that makes public one's most intimate thoughts and experiences. Moreover, they are too often exposed to the use of violence as a means to settle conflict. The consequences of all these dynamics for this generation are far more impactful. Drift itself can have serious implications

What we need are more professionals who understand these dynamics and are able and willing to stand in the gap and intervene in this vortex. Hobson stood in that gap and hopefully many others will as well. He is the right individual to pen this book and share his insights.

Who should read this book?

Academics interested in visual manifestations of drift described from the SRO's perspective;

School Administrators who may be interested in the critique of school disciplinary policies from the SRO perspective;

Parents with children involved in the public school system who are not aware of good kids and not so good kids engaging in *drift*;

Law Enforcement Officers who serve as SROs;

Teachers who are interested in gaining more insight into how students on the edge of *drift* think and how teachers might gain their attention; and

Anyone who enjoys interesting books about real problems.

This book honors "thinking out of the box" and getting out of one's comfort zone. It is about not merely enforcing rules and policies, but investing in the lives of young people. If you are interested in alternatives to business as usual—you will be happy you read this book. Not much is written about School Resource Officers from their perspectives. *Drifters* is an eye-opening account about the world of the public school student—its innocence, turbulence and potential for both good and bad and the SRO as an agent of change. SROs are a critical resource to both students and school administrators. I am grateful that Jack wrote this book. Personally, I hope that there are many more Jack Hobsons out there—standing in the gap, saving—as much as possible—the future of our youth who find themselves in *drift*. – *Carolyn Petrosino, Ph.D.*

PREFACE

A Glimpse Back Through My Rearview Mirror

Aristotle once said that to understand anything, you look at the beginning.

My grandfather once told me that if you find a job you love, make it a career and you'll never work a day in your life.

ℰↈℰↈ

September 1976: My journey to find that special job took me to a university in Miami, Florida, where I learned about the effects of beer, sun, and beach sand on my naive eighteen-year-old psyche. It was my first time away from home. Nevertheless, in my spare time, I studied the Administration of Justice.

January 1979: I entered the Massachusetts Department of Corrections Officers' Training Academy. I graduated and, at twenty-one, five-foot-six and 125 pounds soaking wet, I found myself pacing within a maximum security cell block. It was a solitary job, except for my 24 friends who called Block 16B their home. I was called a hack, a hog, a pig, a screw, and a bull. They watched me, and I watched them plan and scheme. That's the way it was.

January 1985: I entered the Police Academy and took a job with a small town police department. I loved everything about law enforcement, and I knew that time spent with maximum security inmates gave me a unique perception of street patrol. But I had an affinity for education, so I became a DARE (Drug Abuse Resistance Education) Officer.

September 2007: I became an SRO (a school resource officer). I patrolled the high school hallways looking for "Knuckleheads," my slang for kids who did stupid things, said stupid things, and cruised through high school by making stupid decisions. They represented that one percent of trouble-makers, my bad seeds sprouting toward delinquency.

July 2011: After more than three decades in criminal justice, I retired as a police officer. Long before bullying became a tragically iconic buzz word, and long before school shootings rocked the consciousness of the nation, I wanted to write a book about juvenile delinquency—a book about high school and those who inhabit it.

လာလ

I hope you enjoy reading *Drifters* as much I enjoyed writing it. Fasten your seatbelts. – *Dr. Jack Hobson*

INTRODUCTION

Jack

Girl fights, boy fights, sex in bathrooms, classroom rebellions, pranks, drugs, and alcohol. In three decades of working as a police officer and being an integral part of a school system south of Boston, I saw it all.

In 1999, the Columbine tragedy—something that nobody ever guessed would happen in this country— changed the way schools looked at security. That year, the necessity of a School Resource Officer became apparent. A school was now officially part of a cop's beat. It was part of mine. The same year as Columbine, I wrote my doctoral dissertation on bullying, long before that term became a buzzword.

So there I was, quite an anomaly, an experienced and unpretentious cop with a doctorate in education, working in a new cutting-edge high school. This book covers those years and those students. Most of all, it deals with those who drifted across the line toward juvenile delinquency, and with my efforts to push them back.

There's a myth among cops that they know everything, that working the streets and dealing with people in crisis, over time, gives them an edge, a second sense, something more than a hunch. I never bought into that myth, and I dismissed it altogether after my first day as an SRO.

On that day, a sunny September morning, school had been in session for twelve minutes when a girl was choked and knocked to the ground by her boyfriend. Fifty-nine minutes later, I arrested him. For the next almost seven years, the pace never slowed down. I made more arrests at the high school than I had the previous fifteen years on the street.

Whether I was patrolling a neighborhood, walking the halls of a school, or doing my professor stand-up at the university I was fascinated by the psychology of causation, what stages a person went through to become what they are now. To that end, I studied the many ideas considered within Drift Theory of Juvenile Delinquency. Drift Theory contends that impressionable kids drift this way and that, good and bad, until they've committed an offense, or until someone like me comes along to reel them in.

Delinquency prevention begins with two people: the kid who is drifting and the person who recognizes the drift. Two people—the kid and whoever he or she is going to have first contact with. For many in that new, four-story high school, I was that contact. I was the first roadblock on their arduous trek through adolescence, a bumpy and dangerous road littered with bad behavior.

At that school, on a daily basis, it quickly became apparent to me that a considerable amount of juvenile delinquency prevention is just listening. I would very often tell my wayward young friends that their problem was that they talked when they should be listening. I said the same thing to myself—*just listen to the kids*. My goal was to bring all of the theories I had learned into practice. I used one-on-one intervention—frequently under the radar—based on what I knew about juvenile makeup and on what I believed were the needs of each kid. Frequently, it worked out. Sometimes not. However, I believe we were all better for having had that contact. I was often successful because I learned how to make connections with kids who were drifting, and I tried to be there when they veered into the darkness of dangerous and unhealthy decisions. I dealt with each student as an individual and focused on their singular behavior or questionable decisions. The school viewed students through a broader telescope. I weighed my options within what I considered was in a student's best and future interests, according to my plan and all of its fifty-one shades of discretion.

Sometimes they liked me, sometimes they loathed me. But more ran toward me than away. I did everything I could to keep these kids out of trouble. I tried to think ahead for them.

Most would greet me respectfully, others—my works in progress—would acknowledge me as the cop, Jack, Fuzz, Mr. Jack, Five-O, Dude, or with the contemptuous question: "Hey, Jack, do you smell bacon?"

I would reply, "Did you just call me a pig?" Then I would explain that PIG stands for pride, integrity, and guts. Those were the words I needed them to hear.

If they'd committed a minor violation of school rules, I would often ease up a bit on the consequences. I respected and admired the school's administration, but I thought many of the rules were outdated and petty— somewhat trivial in the way discipline was handed out so quickly and by-the-book. I was no stranger to swift justice. I mention this only because prior to my SRO assignment for the school district, I worked in a different world, an alternate universe. I was a patrolman, a street cop, where reality ruled and consequences were often dire. Debates about guilt or innocence happened within the theater of the courthouse. This was the adult world.

But with budding delinquent behavior, consequences might affect future opportunities, including matters pertaining to trust and character, so if I could help it, I preferred to hold court in my office. My jury often consisted of guidance counselors or teachers and, at times, if the behavior was a serious breach of the schools code of behavior, a parent. I practiced restorative justice—the art of the deal—using compromise and leverage, but there was always a price to pay: punishment consistent with the particular school rule violation.

I didn't want a kid to check that box on a job application that started with, "Have you ever been convicted?" I didn't want one of them, on their first job interview, to be excluded because of a past indiscretion. Stealing hotdog or a cookie from the cafeteria was hardly worth the black mark of a larceny charge on a student's criminal history. I knew they'd be applying to college. I didn't want a stupid decision in high school to stop them from getting what they deserved in life.

The principal, vice principals, and faculty played by the rules, and they excelled at keeping all the plates spinning. I had some latitude, although I dropped a few plates. My juggling act was less complicated. I was always trying to think ahead for my drifting students. They were my chess pieces, and I studied them carefully. I didn't enjoy losing.

How easy would it have been to insulate myself behind the badge and project my ideas—and ideals exclusively from a law enforcement point of view—a view that considered arrest as the only option? How seamless and unforgiving would it have been to take the law into my own hands and pass off misbehaving kids to the juvenile court? Let the court figure out their personal and intricate malfunctions. But I knew that the court system doesn't work that way, and painting juveniles with that metaphorical big brush often paints over the problem. It leaves the surface clean, but the damage underneath survives. I understood that, and I loved a challenge.

Many police officers measure their job performance and success statistically: number of arrests, court appearances, calls for service. In this sense, their worth is judged procedurally. And it's linear. I just wanted to help struggling kids, one at a time. I wanted to recognize their behavior before their personal and unpredictable drift began. Measurements and statistical data do not work well in assessing the overactive and ever-changing teenage psyche. Statistics don't have a pulse. Children do, and their hearts beat with zeal and anticipation to different drummers. They are anything but linear, hence their drift.

If I saw kids doing something they shouldn't, I'd steer them into my office and deal with their behavior through mild persuasion, hoping they'd feel a little guilt or shame. I understood that if they were sent to the principal, vice principal, or adjustment counselor, they would be dealt with more harshly. For them, it could mean detention or suspension. More likely than not, parents would become involved. That could result in misunderstandings, each side calling foul. That's why I rarely added parents to the equation.

Teachers, principals, assistant principals, guidance counselors, and adjustment counselors are the life blood of any school. I never envied them their jobs. I had my own style in dealing with kids causing trouble. I was always big with handing out notes, nothing lengthy, just one word, such as *Knucklehead.* I'd give the student one of my small notices, and that would usually stop the trouble. I was no angel in high school, either and, in some strange way, I felt connected to those students, having been in their place thirty-five years before.

Columbine was always tucked back into the dark places in our minds. We were trained to know what to do in the event another school shooter struck or critical incident happened. It was called active shooter training. Take the fight to the suspect. Eliminate the threat with great prejudice. Fast, instinctual, and brutal, if necessary. I checked doors and made sure cameras were working. But prevention was still the best course of action. In concert with emergency services and first responders, we would conduct training exercises—hard lockdowns and soft lockdowns—out in the open, in plain view of students and staff. And we would coach them. We would help them practice their specific roles and responsibilities in the event of a critical incident within the school, like an active shooter. I earned the trust of students and teachers alike because we were bound to a common cause and that cause was our safety. This holistic approach to prevention training was a shared experience.

I always talked to everybody and listened to them. I would tell stories and stupid jokes. Earning the trust of my young rebels gave me instant membership in the confession club. Not the spiritual type. Instead, it was the *Okay, Officer Hobson, I did it, but I can explain* club. As a member of the club, I was entitled to hear all about their problems at home—too many problems, out of the mouths of babes, so to speak. But I listened viscerally and absorbed everything. We got used to each other as our common goals became aligned.

These kids don't spell the word LOVE the way the dictionary does.

They spell it TIME. Almost all of the characters in this book spent too little constructive time with a parent or guardian. Most craved attention and demanded to be recognized, to be heard. When these basic needs were not realized, their personal delinquent-drift began as they traversed that rocky road through adolescence.

For many, I became a surrogate for attachment lost. They saw me as a concerned adult—reliable, and ever-present. And, because I was a police officer, they gravitated slowly to me. I was strict but fair, and I always listened. I would mediate the most absurd differences with understanding, humor, and a grain of salt. "A modern day Solomon," I was called once—probably because in a fit of exasperation, I threatened to tear a boy in half and give equal parts to his warring, jealous girlfriends.

Beginning in the early 1990s, as a DARE Officer and Instructor, I was trained to facilitate parent workshops. I would create age-appropriate sessions for concerned adults in many areas, ranging from adolescent drug use to issues dealing with the teenage rebellion and/or their problems with self-esteem. I would talk about the best practices from selected research, and we'd discuss to how to act and react to deviant and defiant children. This was intended to help empower parents as they navigated their way along the often bumpy road through their children's adolescence. I would suggest to my parent groups that, when their kids were having problems, it might be because they weren't given the time they needed when they needed it, during critical developmental periods in their lives. But the critical periods, the ones that scream "teachable moments," are elusive. So we would discuss how to be a consistent presence in every aspect of their lives.

Consistency and awareness is a two-way street. Doing nothing to correct insolent or defiant behavior only reinforces it. I would have parents dissect their day from the time they got up then dissect their kids' day. Many didn't really have a grip on their kids' daily in-school routine, from the time they got on the school bus until they came home for supper and got yelled at because Dad or Mom had a bad day. Many parents were overscheduled, and their children suffered for it. Children were overscheduled, and their parents suffered for it. A circular problem—different characters, same result.

Many students were latchkey kids, with no adult to greet them or supervise them after school. They were on their own and wandering, like helium balloons, untethered, waiting to drift. I told parents that they needed the ears of a therapist, the eyes of an artist, and the heart of a friend. They had to be strict, fair, and flexible. They had to be a safety net for their kids. They needed a short rope and the skills to use it. We talked collectively but made personal plans for individual problems.

Juveniles drift in and out of deviance, bouncing back and forth between conventional and delinquent lifestyles. Sometimes delinquents feel guilty about their actions and, for the most part, they admire and respect honesty and law-abiding behavior. The lack of social controls in their teenage years allows experimental drifts of activity, good to bad, bad to good. Most grow out of this behavior and level off. Others drift away, and their problems become exponentially criminal. The onset of juvenile delinquency is often subtle and furtive.

This book is a chronicle of sorts, a year in the life of an ordinary American High School. As a school-based police officer, my days were never dull, and I kept a diary of my experiences at school with students, faculty, and staff. Students who earned a place in my journal, and in my consciousness, were the characters that brought life, laughs, and stress into every school day.

We professionals know them as the ones who doddle in notebooks, scratch up desks, stick gum where they shouldn't, create drama, cry wolf, and bring fresh ideas to the title of class clown. They tested the strength and the resolve of teachers and parents and me—the school cop. They are the ones that lived internally in yearbooks and ones we never seemed to forget. Regardless of time and generation, they are our usual suspects, the ones who could never stay out of the spotlight, the ones who broke the law and broke hearts. Their stories are the life blood of this chronicled, roller-coaster school year.

Drifters is a collection of stories about my most memorable characters and their tumultuous drifts between the worlds of right and wrong and good and bad. This book is literally about their trials and tribulations, their punishments on a school level and, for some, their follies with the juvenile court system.

But *Drifters* is not only for my Knuckleheads, or their parents. It's intended to be a glimpse of everyday high school life through my eyes and my perception of things. It's about how I acted and reacted to bad behavior.

This book is for everyone and anyone who struggled to survive high school, and it's for those who spent the glory days of high school taking up space in detention or in the principal's office.

CHAPTER 1

The Zoo

There were two classrooms on the third floor that I affectionately called the Zoo. Rooms 324 and 325 contained a variety of students who repeatedly disrupted the school climate with their behavior. It was a refuge for underachievers, knuckleheads, drama queens, and rebels—with or without a cause—and because of their conduct, they were secluded from the mainstream. They were isolated because of deviant behavior, for not meeting their academic potential, or both. There in the Zoo, they would have to step up to the plate and prove their worth in order to return to a normal classroom environment.

Good behavior was rewarded by merit points received by following their individual education plan. Merits were their currency, their ticket out. The Zoo was located at the end of the hall. I don't know if that was by design, or if those were the only rooms available. For a while, those students were banished to the land of misfit toys.

Public school policies, rules, and behavior codes intersect with criminal law and juvenile law in convoluted ways. It's a delicate dance, more of a chess game really. These worlds collided precariously in that new high school on Massachusetts Bay south of Boston. Although I was at the school daily and witnessed all kinds of insolent behavior, I didn't hand out discipline. I was there to protect, not chastise, but I always added my two cents worth, welcome or not.

As a police officer in full uniform, I did sit in on hearings. I aligned myself with the school administration and represented a useful deterrent in their tool box of discipline. When a situation crossed criminal lines, I got involved. Then words like compromise, probation, and the Zoo came into play.

Disruptive kids, when their social skills and academic achievements dwindled, would go into these classrooms for a tune-up, which could take months. The Zoo wasn't entirely remedial. It was an attempt to restore a path of progress for these troubled kids.

In an educational setting, it's called prescriptive teaching, a strategy designed to meet the individual needs of students with learning or behavioral problems. Students targeted for this type of intervention were administered both psychological and academic achievement tests, along with a complete review of the student's case history.

It was to calm down those students who had trouble, were displaying warning signs, or cues of at-risk behavior, so that they could get back into the regular school environment. There were so many kids at one time, they actually had to open up other classrooms. They sat in assigned seats, and the structure was so rigid no one wanted to end up there. It was all about perception and, with this particular group, perception was not, in a word, good. Although they attended classes during the same hours as the regular school, the students in the Zoo had their own, separate lunch time and remained segregated until they wised up. It was much easier to watch them in one place than search for them in the jumble of the cafeteria.

A lot of them were on individual learning plans and in regular classes, but that wasn't the norm. Many of these drifting misfits would have definitely benefited from a professional diagnosis, but their symptoms and behaviors and individual peculiarities, although observed, were only dealt with on a school level. In this sense, the primary focus in the Zoo was three-fold: re-build trust, behave, and learn.

I was interested in their disciplinary records for clues as to what motivated these students to act out. I would often ask students, "Hey, what's your malfunction? Do you know what etiquette means, because you're really bad at it?"

The most common response was, "What?"

Let me mention one thing here. The nickname I gave the Zoo was no reflection on the teachers who played a continuous game of tug of war to keep the peace, an exhaustive and emotional battle. These kids would threaten, swear, and taunt their teachers. They got into fights. They made text and Facebook threats. They perfected teasing and bullying. Even though they were in the Zoo because they'd caused trouble, they would use their cell phones and various other devices to text and instant message their friends in the general population, the way inmates do—until we changed the rules and locked up their gadgets. Many students were numb from the neck up and made little effort unless it was in being obnoxious and disruptive.

I once heard a psychologist disclose that many of our Zoo inhabitants experienced flare-ups of ODD, Oppositional Defiant Disorder. My translation: Bratty teenagers reliving their terrible twos who perfected tantrums and revolted against rules of any kind, so much so that even the most menial of requests became skirmishes. Through my eyes, they were Knuckleheads.

Just so you understand, here are a few credos—my precepts regarding that rare state. You might be a Knucklehead if:

• You're a sixteen-year-old boy and, by mistake, take your baby sister's Hello Kitty backpack to school and are forced to physically defend yourself against relentless taunts.

• You punch the emergency exit on the inside ceiling of the school bus, and it blows out skyward like a pilot's ejector seat.

• You bring a whoopee cushion to class, one that actually smells like rancid expelled gas, and cause a mini laugh riot when the teacher becomes your first, and only, victim.

• You have to go to the school nurse because, on a dare, you rubbed Icy Hot on your private parts.

• You steal a tarantula from the biology department, place in on the shoulder of your ex-friend who, in a panic, brushes it off and stomps down hard, killing the two-hundred-fifty dollar spider.

• You throw a carton of milk down the staircase to trip someone and fall yourself, face-first, and need stitches.

• Between classes, you brush your teeth with hemorrhoid cream.

• While riding your skateboard in the hall, you fall off and, sliding, you become a human bowling ball, students and teachers become bowling pins, and for the first time in your life, you roll a strike.

Get the picture? Girls are as eligible for knucklehead status as boys. Life *and* *I* don't discriminate. A Knucklehead girl might wear pajama bottoms and flip-flops to school regardless of weather conditions.

"What's a few inches of snow on my feet?" was a common response. "Hobson, it ain't *nothing*."

Add to the female Knucklehead recipe a couple of Facebook hate clubs with a dash of social hostility. Combine a healthy dose of love and hate relationships—gender not specific—that burn hot on the school bus but fizzle to smoke by lunch time. Mix this with defiance, seasoned with a dab of apathy, and you have a dodgy, slightly undeveloped rebel princess. Priceless.

The Zoo residents were indeed Knuckleheads, and I was called there repeatedly to chat with my usual suspects. I would remove the obnoxious students, counsel the stupid, confine the aggressive, and compliment and reinforce good behavior. Always.

Arrest was a last resort, as in driving-the-angels-crazy last resort. I would take the accused for a walk, get some fresh air, and talk about what happened. I would buy him or her a soda, hand over a mint or a piece of gum, a gesture of inclusion, simple and innocuous.

We would talk about nonsense: the Red Sox, the weather, our favorite TV shows. By the time I brought the kid back, more often than not, he or she was calm again. I enjoyed their company and was always fascinated by their thought processes, their rationalization of decisions, wise and not so wise. Baffling sometimes, but never dull.

I had a lot of inherent authority in the schools. If something happened, the principal would often seek my advice. That was always a two-way street. They knew how to handle problems and issues from the school's perspective of due process, and I knew more about the quagmire of the juvenile courts. We were successful in maintaining that delicate balance. Having the police and the schools reading the same book was triumphant, though getting us all on the same page proved daunting at times. But our tenacity and differences were not ego driven. Our energy was reserved for the students.

We had a truant officer who dealt with kids who came in late or not at all. Although we were allies, our roles were different. Every morning, after we shut the doors for the day, and all of the kids were supposed to be there, I'd tell the guidance counselor, "I'm going out fishing for a while. I'll be back in about an hour."

She'd smile because everyone knew what I meant. I wasn't casting for fish. Instead, I'd go cruising, looking for the walkers. I was seeking out my usual suspects, many of them Zoo kids, an interesting and rag-tag mix of unmotivated travelers. The walking dead.

I would find them, looking like zombies in their pajamas, some in the same clothes they'd worn the day before, heading in the direction of school, some alone, some in small groups, drinking black coffee. I'd pick them all up. Sometimes, I'd have five kids in the back of the cruiser.

"What time did you go to bed? Why can't you get up in the morning? Did you eat something? Did you all remember to bring your medication?" I'd ask. "Why can't you get your ass here on time? Everyone else does. Stay awake, go inside, find a book, and open it—that would be an accomplishment. Learn something, for Christ's sake. Don't be a Knucklehead."

They would smile and yawn and look at me with vacant eyes because they'd heard this rant before, many times.

I'd pull up to the front door of the school. The truant officer would be waiting. I'd let the kids out, and she'd let them in. A tardy they could deal with, but if they were marked absent, which they would be after eight o'clock, the penalties accumulated, and discipline was progressive and harsh.

"How many fish did Jack catch today?" someone in the office would ask the truant officer.

"Oh, he did pretty well. Four or five."

That wasn't part of the job. It was just part of what I did because my focus wasn't just about preventing trouble. It was thinking about the kids.

Many of the young men and women you'll get to know in this book spent time in the Zoo. Had it existed when I was a kid growing up in Brockton, I probably would have spent time there as well. When, years later, I wrote a grant for an alternative high school in our community, I was thinking about those kids, thinking about their limited opportunities. Knucklehead status isn't terminal. It doesn't have to be a life sentence. That's what the Zoo—and the kids who resided there—taught me.

CHAPTER 2

Alex: The Crawler

Alex was a prime candidate for the Zoo, and he was one of the first students diagnosed with Oppositional Defiant Disorder I met on my job. On a crisp, sunny day in October, I received a call from the school's principal, Kristen McKay. Though it was still early in the school year, Alex, already a troubled student, had become out of control again. Now his mother had stormed into Kristen's office very upset. Could I come down and help out? Being the administration's go-to guy in those situations, I began my trip from the third floor down to the first, remembering that this particular mother was the definitive "helicopter parent," one who continually hovered over her child, waiting to crash down and protect him during a crisis.

When I arrived on the scene, the irate mother was telling the principal that the reason her son was having trouble was because the teachers couldn't keep up with him. "He's so intelligent," she shouted, "He should be in a special class."

I knew this kid. He had been in therapy since elementary school and possessed the vocabulary of a psychologist, coupled with the emotions of a child. He could express what he felt was wrong with others, and he did, spontaneously, but he couldn't prevent his own meltdowns. Certainly, what he'd been telling his mother at home about his time here in school was far from the truth.

Kristen didn't raise her voice as she calmly faced the irate mother. "Alex is prone to tantrums," she said. "He needs to be placed in a special social environment where he can improve his studies and level out his behavior. The next time Jack here has to be called in, your son will be suspended."

That's when I spoke up. "He'll be placed there until he learns not to be disruptive," I said, recognizing the mother. At one time she had driven a bus for handicapped kids near my neighborhood.

She remembered me, too. "I don't want the police talking to my son for any reason whatsoever," she said, "not unless I'm there."

I'd heard that a few times. It was a common response.

"Jack is our School Resource Officer," Kristen informed her.

I tried to match her calm demeanor. "I'm here for the safety of the staff and students both. Alex needs to improve his attitude before returning to his regular classes." I was careful not to use the word "Zoo" while mentioning the classrooms upstairs.

Outside the windows, the day had turned gray. *Typical,* I thought. Sunshine followed by half a foot of snow. Alex's mouth had gotten him in trouble, and he was a royal pain in the ass. His behavioral portfolio listed him as suffering from multiple phobias and syndromes. But I always thought there was hope for the kid. I was about to relay that message to his mom, but she started for the door in a huff. Mom was like a bad penny, always around and always underfoot, threatening mayhem and vile consequences if her demands were not met.

"I'll go to an advocacy group and get him tested," she shouted. "He should be enrolled in a special individual education plan, and he needs a class where he can showcase his skills."

Oh, we have just the place, I thought with a smile.

A couple of days, maybe a week later, I got a report that Alex had sworn at a teacher and refused to open a book in class. He'd become surly and wouldn't even try to complete an assignment. He was being a wise ass and, on that particular day, he was riling up the other students. The class environment bordered on anarchy. At this rate, he'd never get out of the Zoo. The teacher was at her wit's end and requested that I remove Alex from class.

In that class, you got rewarded points for settling into a routine, completing your work on time, and being cooperative. Once students accumulated enough points, they could return to their regular classes.

A few minutes later, I was at the door to his classroom, my arms folded in front of my chest. There was Alex crawling on the floor like a crab, the others kids roaring with laughter.

"The police, the police," he shouted, looking up at me. "You can't come in. My mother says I don't have to talk to you."

The female teacher, a veteran who could usually handle bad behavior, gave me a look I'd become familiar with. Alex had gone beyond her limit. "What do we do with him?" she asked.

"Put all the other kids in the room next door," I said.

This took some time, but soon we were alone with Alex.

The teacher was exhausted. "Do we call the nurse, Jack?"

"Not yet," I said, watching Alex crawl among the seats on all fours. "Check on the kids next door and give me some time alone with him."

When she looked back at me from the doorway, I gestured for her to lock the door. Once she had left, I pulled up a chair in front of the classroom and waited him out. A good twenty minutes passed. Finally, he rose to his feet and bolted for the door.

Yanking the handle, he began to scream. "Let me out. I'm being held captive. I've been kidnapped. Somebody help me."

I got out of my chair and walked toward him. He began to tremble, cowering as if he expected a blow. When I reached his side, I spoke softly into his ear. "If you don't sit the fuck down, I'm going to break your neck." The old policeman whisper-in-your-ear trick.

It worked. Alex sat down in a chair. I settled in one next to him. "I'm not really going to break your neck." I gave him a moment. "And I'm not going to tell your mother what happened here today."

He didn't ask why, but I could see questions in his eyes.

"I'm going to try and get you into another class, Alex," I said, trying a ploy that I hoped wouldn't backfire. "You're too smart to be here in this room, crawling around on the floor like you were raised in the jungle."

After a long pause, I got up and motioned for him to follow. When I unlocked the door and ushered him out into the hall, it was empty. All the kids had already been to lunch and had returned to their classrooms. I began walking. He followed, looking less stressed, as if he wasn't going to bolt.

Downstairs, the cafeteria was closing, but I led him into the facility and up to the food service line. "Look at this stuff," I said. "It's all still looking fresh. What would you like?"

Alex gave me a sour look. "I'm not hungry."

"I'm buying."

"Really?"

I almost laughed as he took my bait, using the oldest trick to get a teen to cross over and join the enemy. He loaded his plate with spaghetti and meatballs, chicken nuggets, a hamburger, and Jell-O. I picked out something light. My stomach was churning, but not from hunger. I was still upset by his behavior, and now I had ruled out all the dire consequences he deserved. Instead of grabbing seats in the cafeteria, a place more kids would soon be taking over, I directed Alex into the faculty lounge.

"Let's try it in here," I said.

He gave me a look of amazement, like was I sure I wanted him in there? I watched him while he ate, each bite accompanied by a look around the empty room. In time, I saw him become more at ease. After a few minutes, we were talking baseball, what shows we watched on TV, all the safe subjects.

Time passed, and he began to fidget. I figured it must be time for another dose of Good Cop.

"Come with me," I said.

"Where we going?"

"Another office where we won't be bothered."

It was easy to see he didn't quite trust me, but he dutifully trekked after me into another vacant room and sat at a computer station.

"You can't go on Facebook," I informed him.

"Can I play a video game?"

I booted up the computer. "Sure, go ahead."

I got comfortable and watched him out of half-closed eyes, allowing him to have a bit of time away from the immensity of the school and all the pressure it could push down on a student. After a while, he sat back and grinned. "I better get going," he said. "My mom's picking me up."

I pictured a helicopter dipping down to hover over the school's front steps. "I'll walk with you, my friend."

We walked outside. There were patches of snow here and there. The sun was showing itself low in the sky. No helicopter, but his mother was waiting for him outside her SUV.

"What's my son doing with you?" she demanded, glaring at me, her voice close to hysterical.

"No reason," I said. "We just happened to hit the door together."

I broke off in another direction. Who knew what the kid would say to his mother. Certainly, she'd quiz him. Would I get a call tomorrow from the principal again? What kind of story would Alex tell his mom? Would I be able to keep this assignment long enough to back up my promise to him about offering him special treatment?

Alex seemed to wake up after that day, and I did help get him transferred into a more structured class. And this happened because he started to engage with other students in a relatively positive way. But still he challenged me, getting into trouble a few weeks after straightening out. I took him aside with a few other seniors and threatened him with the padded room the school provided for the autistic kids who were in danger of hurting themselves.

"Up there, you have to go it alone. Even I'm not allowed." I watched as they tried to discern my honesty. Picking out Alex's worried grin, I aimed my words at him. "I'm watching you guys," I added. "Some of you have been to the Zoo. The padded room is much worse."

The group began to point fingers and slap one another on the back. Alex joked with the others, laughing with them at how I'd never get them sent to the padded room. He was with his friends now. No longer was he the crab, crawling on all fours.

Maybe his short stay in the Zoo had helped change him.

I filed a report about the crawling incident, if for no other reason than it would cover me if any in that room of witnesses should challenge my demeanor.

"This is fine, Jack," Principal Kristen McKay said, "but in the future, keep these things to yourself, okay?"

I didn't tell her what I did keep to myself. As the year went on, Alex's mother would poke her head into my office now and then.

"How are you doing, Jack" she'd ask in a friendly voice that had no resemblance to her previous helicopter self. I took that to mean Alex was better. I also took it to mean the Zoo had actually done some good.

〰〰〰

Afterthoughts:

First, nobody knows their kids better than parents...well, let's clarify that, *involved* parents. That said, parents and guardians, brothers and sisters are on the frontline, and changes in a child's behavior that cause battles of insolence, anger, and strife within the family will most likely happen at home. And the family will bear the brunt of these changes and deal with them accordingly. If the cycle of bad acts and deeds makes it to school, then they will be observed by teachers, students, and probably me—the SRO. If this behavior is repeated and causes disruption of normal daily activities or interrupts academic objectives, then a plan and a team might be the next step, a strategic plan, short of an intervention or alternative school placement. Time for an assessment—a check list of symptom, options, and ideas.

Alex learned the language of doctors and therapists long before he learned to read. He would rattle off acronyms directed at me and my behavior. We had a running joke. Most of the school staff started their work day with a donut and coffee. I started mine with a diagnosis from Alex and my horoscope. He forecasted more than a few of my bad days—the ones in which he was a deliberate Knucklehead. He was a classic instigator—a troubled kid, causing trouble. He did it intentionally, and he seemed to enjoy it. I never thought he was a dummy.

Alex showed some growth after we came into each other's lives. He seemed to be adjusting to his surroundings and was earning decent but not stellar grades. I was cautious in thinking that he might be in the process of growing out of his defiant behavior, but now and then, he would have a little skirmish with another kid or tell a teacher to go and pound tar, so we kept in touch.

Alex's battles on the home front with his parents and brothers and sisters were continuous. His mother would call me to vent or to talk or to ask me what would happen to her if Alex suddenly disappeared off the face of the planet. I told her that wasn't a good plan because wherever he went, they'd kick him out and send him back.

I asked her to give me an example of Alex's household behavior because he was fairly calm at school within the boundaries of his academic plan and with me watching him like a hawk.

She told me a story about the difference between an ODD kid and children with other phobias and disorders.

She said that a teenager diagnosed with ADHD or ADD, or any other included acronym, if shut into a room for punishment, most likely would kick and bang and scream until they were exhausted.

If locked in a room, ODD kids, like Alex, would break out the window and escape leaving a trail of destruction, breaking things that might piss off other family members, like his brothers and sister. That was his way of defiance—getting even, not giving in. He would never stray far from home and would return, usually silent and tired. The current battle had ended, but tomorrow was another day.

I thought that was just awesome.

CHAPTER 3

The First Steps: Harry

Let me tell you about my very first walk with a student. As the years ticked on, these treks inside of schools, and out, morphed into one-on-one interventions—personal talks about personal things, questions and answers to questions, my ideas and their reactions, my point of view and their point of view. You can learn so much in thirty minutes.

I am the SRO for an entire school district, so issues or problems with any grade level are part of my responsibilities. Each spring, after DARE graduation for grades K-3, I begin my curriculum at the middle school, our intermediate grades. Middle school, if you remember, can be a raucous place inhabited by boys and girls struggling to understand why biology has changed their bodies, their urges, and their perception of things. And, middle school age is usually the age when kids know so much more than their parents and once loving mothers and fathers are reduced to common idiots who are suddenly, *persona non grata*. These were indeed the roller coaster years, and nothing that could happen inside this middle school would surprise me—or so I thought.

Our middle school housed grades four through eight, ages approximately 8 to 14. Harry was in the fourth-grade when I first met him. He was the first autistic student I had dealt with as a police officer. On the day we met, Harry had punched another student, a fourth-grade girl named Becky. Now Becky was somewhat of a tomboy and slugged Harry back, leaving a small cut on his face and a bruised ego. The principal asked me to intervene and negotiate the terms of punishment, or surrender in this case.

"Okay, a fight between 10 year-olds? Why am I even here?" I asked the principal.

"Well, one of the students, a boy, is new to this class and this is his first day. Some parents are not happy with him being in class with their children," he said in an apologetic tone.

"Where's this boy now?" I asked.

"With the janitor in his office," he said.

"Why isn't he with the nurse or in the assistant principal's office? What are you not telling me, Frank?"

"Follow me," he said.

As we entered the janitor's office, Mike the janitor and a longtime friend of mine was arm-wrestling with this other person, his back to me, but clearly an adult and a big one at that.

"What's up guys," I asked.

Frank said to the boy, "Harry, this is Officer Hobson. He wants to talk to you about something. Okay?"

Damn, I thought, *this kid is huge. He could catch geese with a rake.* Looking him over, I asked, "Harry, how old are you, my friend?"

Harry looked at me and said, "Is that a real gun? Can I hold it? Have you ever shot anyone? How big is that badge? About three inches? It's shiny."

Rapid fire questions, like a television changing channels indiscriminately. Harry stood and approached me with somewhat of a limp. Standing up he was a least a foot taller than I was.

I put out my hand and he shook it.

"Hi," is all he said.

We talked about what happened in the classroom. Harry seemed to be totally disconnected from the little dust up with the girl. I asked the principal if I could take Harry for a walk, outside, for some fresh air.

Before he could answer, Harry became very upset and started to pace back and forth in this already cramped office. "No walk, no walk, no walk, no walk," he repeated over and over with growing intensity.

I didn't understand. Had I said something wrong?

He started to whine, saying, "Can I go home now? I want to go home now, and can I go home?"

"What's up, Frank, what's happening?" I said.

"Harry's father should be here in a few minutes. We'll talk to him about our next step."

What next step, I thought, and how this incident is a police problem? Two ten-year-olds had a little push-and-shove, hardly an issue at all.

Harry's father seemed like a nice guy, caring and very protective, and I knew where Harry got his height.

He was apprised of the dust-up in the classroom and sighed. "Harry's just trying to adjust. This is all new to him. He'll settle down?"

That sounded more like a leading question, I thought, *one in which you reach for the answer you want, as if hearing a kernel of understanding from someone else's mouth gets it out of your head and makes it real.* We talked together for a while and I learned more about Harry and his autism, his tantrums, and violent outbursts. I had a better understanding as to why some parents didn't want him mainstreamed with their kids. Today was to be Harry's first experience in a regular classroom.

I asked Harry's dad if on occasion I could take him outside for a walk.

Dad stunned me by saying that, "Only if you tether him—a restraint we have used since his growth spurt last year—6 inches and 25 pounds, almost overnight. He's very strong now, and strong-willed. If he runs, he'd be hard to stop. And he limps a bit, too much pressure on his growth plate, and he cries when he's tired or in pain," he said.

"I noticed the limp," I told Dad. "Okay, tether him—do you mean like a leash, so when I say I'll take him for a walk, you literally mean that I'll walk him?"

"It's the only way we'd be comfortable with you taking him outside, police officer or not."

But my law enforcement intuition begged the question: *Do they crate this kid, too*?

Wow, that was a new one, I thought, recalling the old saying, Don't judge someone until you've walked a mile in their shoes, or moccasins, or something like that.

What I failed to understand at the time was that my initial involvement with Harry was not the principal's idea. It was Harry's dad's. Shortly after the "punch in the classroom," the special needs teacher called Harry's father, in compliance with their protocol. The father in turn called the principal and asked if I was in the building. I was their preemptive strike. It seemed that they were several steps ahead of the other parents and, apparently, they felt that aligning with me gave them an advantage if push came to shove over Harry remaining in the program. I suppose it did, on some level, but this kid only had one strike against him and, in my view of things, you're still at the plate with one strike.

Harry went home with Dad and stayed home for a couple of days. When he returned to school, I was asked to sit in on his reentry hearing. As it turned out, my presence had been recommended by Harry's school psychologist, not for my understanding of kids in crisis, but for my calming influence working with students with special problems under special circumstances. I spoke with both Mom and Dad this time and, after a very long conversation about all things Harry, they acquiesced and allowed me to take him for walks from time-to-time, but only inside the school.

Our walks became a common sight and a target for good-natured jokes and laughter. We were never fazed, at least Harry wasn't. Here's a visual—foghorn leghorn, the giant cartoon rooster with a southern, good ole' boy style and a penchant for mischief with his tiny, very chatty adversary, the chicken hawk, walking and talking. We made an odd couple.

Our conversations were spontaneous, and we mostly talked about what we saw and what we heard along the way: papers and trash on the floor, colorful posters on the walls, dented school lockers, the occasional student in the hall running an errand. We heard all the sounds of teachers and students, hushed behind closed doors; voices over the intercom; yelling from somewhere; laughter; and the outside sounds of car horns, fire engine sirens, and birds. I became very attached to this gentle giant of a ten-year-old. We would walk around the school when classes were in session and the halls were empty. We always visited Mike the janitor because he was Harry's friend, and he allowed the boy to tinker with his tools, scotch tape, and molding putty. And if Harry was good, Mike would show him how to make and cut keys.

Harry and I walked at least once a month for the next three school years and, when school was not in session, I would stop by his house in my police cruiser and visit.

We walked all the time, right up until the day he left middle school in the eighth grade for a group home setting and a new school.

He's 14 years old now and doing well in his new school. We e-mail a lot. I even scolded him more than once about the dangers of the web. He told me that I needed to grow up and get a life. Ouch!

With Harry by my side, I took the very first step on what would become a long and very rewarding journey.

CHAPTER 4

The Birth of an Urban Legend

As pleased as I was that Alex was finding his own way through school, I was concerned with little pockets of violence that made no sense to me.

And they were coming from a school bus.

Bus 13.

The symbolic meaning of number 13 has roots over 2000 years old: 12 disciplines plus one, 13. The Knights Templar—knights empowered by God to protect his sacred relics, were considered invincible—but they were captured and many burned on the stake on Friday, October13, 1307. The first American flag had 13 stars and 13 stripes to represent the 13 original colonies. Dante Alighieri, the Renaissance poet, wrote *Dante's Inferno*, the story of his epic journey through hell that began on the "Thursday of Mysteries," the second Thursday in April 1300. Pick your favorite number 13 superstition—we all have one.

For various reasons, I found myself on a school bus nearly every day. They were old carriage buses, type four, built in 1975 like a tank, and carried 45 students. Each bus existed in its own world, its own universe. They were carriages full of stories: Kids stealing lunches. Kids sitting on kids. Kids tormenting and being tormented. Kids divided by age and every conceivable cultural divide, though there were no assigned seats on the buses. No seat belts either. The Motor Vehicle Code makers, in their infinite wisdom, had decided the seat in front of a passenger acted as a kind of buffer in case of an accident. So it was in the norm to find students sitting three deep in preferred sections. As in the classrooms and the cafeteria, kids would gravitate toward the most devilish hot spots, where all their energy could boil up, mile after mile.

The bus drivers, mostly retired truckers and some very seasoned, good-natured women, were a tough lot who stuck to their seats, hands on the wheel. My first encounter with Bus 13 was early in the school year on a cool September morning. I was called over my police radio and dispatched to a car-versus-school-bus accident. Upon arrival, I discovered that Bus 13 had been sideswiped by a pick-up truck and was disabled. No injuries. As I helped transfer the students to another bus, a young boy—about 13—slipped and fell on the stairs. He landed on his tailbone and was taken by ambulance to the hospital.

It was the bus driver's job was to obey the rules of the road. They were not—by law or by choice—to act as boxing or wrestling referees, let alone guidance counselors. If they observed trouble in their big rear view mirror, they were to call their respective schools for help. However, the occasional threat, repeated often and with ear-shattering accuracy by the driver, was somewhat effective.

But not on Bus 13.

Sam, one of my favorite drivers, called my cell phone one day in early spring and said that everything was tranquil on the home front. It wouldn't be for long.

"Jack, Bus 13's at it again," he said. "We have us a fight going on."

I pictured Sam, a good, old, navy, chain-smoking boy with faded tattoos on his arms, trying to handle a bunch of rowdy misfits while he held on to the road. Sam was an aging biker with a thick chain securing his wallet to his back pocket. I would tease him about the deep lines on his face and he'd tell me that his life adventures consisted of hard miles—all in inches.

"I'm on my way," I said.

The bus drivers were ignored by some, but they were the people who saw the students in a way that few did. Sam was one of the ones I trusted. He could tell me which drivers were drama queens and which ones least tolerated bad behavior.

When I got there, he was waiting outside his bus. A crusty road veteran, he was never fazed by student fights. "I don't do discipline but, Jack, what these kids really need is a..."

"I know, preaching to the choir my friend," I replied, finishing his thoughts of real discipline in my head. "Let's see what we have to deal with here." Sam had kept three boys on board. I addressed them. "What's the problem?"

"We didn't do anything," said the ring leader, all of four feet tall and about 85 pounds of defiance.

A kid back in the shadows showed his face and pointed to the seat I had picked out to lean my hip against. "The kid who was sitting in that seat threw something, and we threw it back."

"And that started all this nonsense?" I asked.

"I guess so," squeaked the little kid in the back. "But we didn't start it," he said, pointing tediously to the back of the bus.

I thought about unlucky Bus 13. Assigned to mostly sophomores and freshmen, it was gaining a bad reputation for trouble. I realized that I was standing where I'd stood before on calls like this.

"This seat right here?" I asked. Suddenly I picked up a scent that sent me reeling. Something smelled rotten, maybe a mouse. Immediately I pivoted and hopped off the bus to talk with Sam. "What's that awful smell in the middle of the bus?"

"Welcome aboard," Sam said dryly as he chewed on a toothpick. "All year I've smelled that. It's terrible. It stays up in your nostrils all day. The kids call this bus the fart mobile."

He and I got back on the bus and went straight to the seat. I searched it high and low, unearthing more of the odor. Finding it moist under the padding, I unstrapped the K-Bar knife from my boot and poked a few holes underneath, here and there. Sam took an exaggerated step back, and in sync two of boys dropped f-bombs.

"It's dripping," I said, yanking my hand back.

I slashed about a six-inch slice of what pretended to be green, polished vinyl along the seat. It was full of mold, and something else that resembled smelly red foam. "Your bus, Sam—" I said, "—has to go in."

Condensation, food spillage, and paranormal overtones had ended Bus 13's reign as the most evil in the carpool. At least for now.

"What do we do?" Sam asked.

"We can call the fire department," I said. *Here we go*, I thought. *What happens if this seat is toxic?*

And it was—to the tune of an $1,100 bill just for testing and other forensics. At least we had found out the reason there were so many fights on Bus 13.

It wasn't because the kids on that bus were so bad. It was because the seat was.

So Bus 13 went back to the special garage for haunted buses, where the influence of bad kids from generations past escaped now and then to push the good kids of today into irrational nonsense.

This would be the fourth exorcism of Bus 13 since 1989, its fourth rebuild and update. Always the same seat, same smell, same aura, same bad vibe every decade.

Urban legend? Instead of Friday the 13th, we had Bus 13.

Come to think of it, the last fight happened on a Friday the 13th. I should have played the lottery. After that fateful day, rumors were rampant and circulated feverishly. The bus became a favorite screen saver on cell phones and computers. A girl reportedly had a seizure and was still in a "bad-seat" coma. Students claimed to have been electrocuted or shocked when sitting there. The seat, many swore, was always many degrees colder than the inside of the bus—paranormally cold, a student told me. After exiting the bus, many who sat in the seat claimed that the seat of their pants was blotched with a purple, sticky, wet substance that oozed like a blood stain and then, just as quickly, would disappear.

And my favorite is that, from time-to-time, the seat thumped in-and-out like a heart.

Urban legend.

CHAPTER 5

An Emotional Mutiny:
Pirates and Police Girls

About the time we were solving the mystery of Bus 13, another calamity struck the campus.

Theme day.

Theme days were held throughout the school year, days where students could dress up and express themselves in accordance to a certain theme. The concept for that day's dress-up was pirates. Though it suggested free-wheeling behavior, things seemed manageable, until three of the school's cheerleaders decided that all pirates liked their women with lots of cleavage and plenty of leg covered in fishnets. Was their choice of attire over the top? Well, the boys were going crazy. It was going to be a close call.

I spied a few crying female pirates when I was walking past the glass-encased Guidance Office on my way to referee a heated argument between two teachers over the use of a microscope. A spectrograph, I was later corrected.

"My spectrograph."

"No, you moron, it's mine and it's a spectroscope. I'll knock your teeth out and stick that sorry excuse for a microscope up your ass."

"Fuck off."

As soon as I realized their f-bombs were inciting their students, I stepped in and suggested they give their jaws a rest.

Crazy, right?

Believe me, students weren't always the problem. I took the microscope and stored it in my office. After a while, their anger subsided. When cooler heads prevailed, I returned the device.

The aftermath of this little dust up between the teachers and my intervention became a concern for the teachers union. They weren't on my side, just the contrary. They were vocal, adversarial, angry, and downright indignant about a police officer taking a microscope out of a biology class. They threatened a grievance, but my retort to the in-house union representative was that I would argue my side of the story in the court of public opinions—the parents. That ended their union action.

After returning the device, I was called to the Guidance Office. I remembered the day before when Kristen, the principal, made an announcement over the school-wide intercom and warned all the young women that slutty pirates would not be tolerated, and offenders would walk the plank all the way home. No exceptions. The crying pirate girls now made more sense.

I quickly learned that very early in the day, one-by-one, teachers were sending the inappropriately dressed girls down to the Guidance Office. Although the costumes were expertly designed and arranged, the diverse male populations of the school, age notwithstanding, were getting a little anxious.

Three girls were captured and confined. Next to be escorted to Guidance was a sexy police officer, wearing a low-cut shirt, tight pants, police belt, and holster, fake gun, handcuffs, and high heels. I was called and was met by the provocative police girl—a friend and frequent flyer of questionable behavior—named Missy.

Missy drifted in and out of the Zoo. She was the type of girl I saw as spoiled and corruptible, but never held accountable for her sins. Popular with every crowd, she existed on the fringe of every clique. Loved by boys. Hated by girls. Tolerated by me.

Her girly charm stonewalled some male teachers, infuriated female teachers, and really tested my nerves. But I liked her. I knew her issues, her family, her problems, her fears, and her insecurities. She was a constant blip on my radar.

Suddenly, Paul, our new dean of students, stormed into the office on a mission, red-faced, neck veins bulging, obviously upset. A quick glance at the girl pirates and female police officer begot an eruption of very loud and totally one-sided anger.

"You were warned," he screamed. "Missy, really. I've been here for a couple of months, and why are you always dressing like you're on a manhunt?"

What a dickhead, I thought. There's nothing worse than an adult—a school administrator at that—attacking a teenage girl's self-esteem with rude, rumor-starting comments.

She shrugged and became immediately defensive. "Anything else, Paul?" she said, calling the dean of students by his first name.

"You're all going home. You're all getting suspended. And not one of you is going to the semi-formal. Do you understand me? Enough is enough."

Panic and tears took over, a veritable mutiny of emotions. Hysterical 911 text messages to parents were fast and furious. This caused unimaginable grief. The news bordered on apocalyptic. The girls began to sob and protest. By this time, several teachers and staff members wanted to know what the commotion was. Pam, a guidance counselor, shocked by the dean's explosive decision, was trying to do damage control.

"Jack, can you do something?" she asked. "Please, talk to him. He'll listen to you." Pam's concern was palpable because she was the coordinator and director of all things semi-formal. "Please, Jack," Pam pleaded. "The semi-formal's tomorrow night."

This called for more than just damage control. I asked Pam to follow me to the school store. The store was run by a parent group who put their profits back into various school programs that lacked funding.

It was closed. But, as the school's resource officer, I had master keys for every door, every file cabinet, and every elevator for security reasons. I opened the door and quickly scooped up a couple of sweatshirt and sweat pant combinations. Then I locked the door and headed for my office. In my file cabinet, I found the stash of lost and found clothing that I'd washed and disinfected. Some stuff I'd hand out to kids needing more to wear than they had put on before leaving home for school. I grabbed a few more sweatshirts and coveralls.

Amidst the crying, was one very pissed off and stoic police girl. I passed her some clothes to cover her bare flesh and tight suggestive apparel.

"This is bullshit, Jack, and you know it," Missy said.

"Not now, Missy. Don't be a wiseass," I told her. "And where did you get the State Police badge you're wearing. It's real, and wearing that is against the law. I'll bet there's a pissed off trooper looking frantically for it."

"Megan gave it to me," she said. "Her father's a trooper."

"Take it off."

"Why don't you take it off for me, Officer Hobson?" she said, seductively.

I knew that when Missy was nervous, she flirted. "Missy, knock that shit off. It won't work with me. And give me that fake gun. I won't even get into how stupid that is. Dangerous, too. Sometimes, I think you're just a broken toy."

She frowned and flashed an obscene gesture my way.

Shaking my head, I snarled, "You are a gem, Missy."

I asked a guidance counselor to call Megan out of class. Megan came to the Guidance Office and I asked her if I should call her dad about the badge, or was she going to be a big girl and take the badge from Missy, take it home, and put it back exactly, and I meant *exactly*, where she found it. I explained that a badge to a police officer represented the job and symbolized our authority and all our protections under the law. "In other words," I reminded her, "police officers know exactly where their badges are at all times. No discussion."

"Okay, okay, I get it," Missy said and gave up the badge.

The pirate girls had also changed their clothing. All the fishnets, cleavage, protruding breast lines, tight pants, and high heels were gone. With the girls covered from head to toe, the tension seemed to drop a notch.

What remained were sugar and spice and everything nice—as nice as a pissed-off swarm of hornets could be. I also learned that somebody had called Roger, the school store manager. And he arrived at the school in great haste. Roger was a retired business owner in town and rumor had it that he ran his business like a dictator.

"You should have talked to me first," he admonished me.

"There wasn't time."

"How did you get in?"

"I used a key," I said, as if that excused the burglary.

"You shouldn't even have a key."

I threw my arm around his shoulder. "Roger, let's go into your store and find out how much money I owe you." As we walked, I tried to soften him up. "What I did was probably wrong, but I couldn't think of any other way to resolve the issue."

Roger gave me the hard news. Although the road to hell is paved with good intentions, my ride cost me two hundred dollars. I tried to guilt Roger into donating the clothing under the circumstances. "Roger, did you know that if we have a critical or dangerous incident at the school, the store is a designated safe haven?"

"No," was all he said.

He wouldn't let it slide.

Parents were starting to arrive in response to the end-of-their-world-as-they-knew-it text messages.

Paul, the Dean of Students, was in a very uncomfortable meeting with a few parents and other concerned teachers and adults. New at the job, he was outnumbered. He was literally backed into a corner. I knew how this had to end and that he was stubborn, but I also knew kids were one thing. Parents, mothers in particular, were another. You only fought the battles you could win, and Paul was a dead-man-walking. But I let him stew a bit, enjoying his uncomfortable scuffle from afar. Usually, I'm in the thick of things. Truth be told, I'd rather wrestle a polar bear than take on a gang of infuriated mothers.

A compromise was negotiated. A truce was declared. The offenders would serve detention. They could stay in school and they could attend the dance.

Parents approached me to thank me for my intervention. I told them that when everyone is happy it makes my job easier. They offered to pay me for the substitute clothing. I declined. I'd take care of that later.

After persistent prodding from Roger to pay for the clothes, I ended his bill-collector harassment and paid the 200 dollars out of my own pocket. Done.

I set up a donation jar on my desk. That appeased many parents who gratefully contributed. If anyone wanted to, they could put money in the jar. I never asked for any money and I never articulated that the jar was for monetary payback regarding the theme-day fiasco, but through word of mouth, students, parents, and staff contributed. However, behind the scenes, I was raising money for a Zoo cookout.

After a week or so, I removed the jar. With the one hundred sixty-six dollars collected, I approached the teacher who controlled the Zoo. I wanted to see if, as a class, they deserved a special event. Can't give away rewards to the unworthy. I knew these kids were segregated and for good reasons, but their classroom had windows, and they could see all the other students outside being rewarded with picnics and cookouts. It wasn't fair to the Zoo kids and they knew it. And on the days when the other students were outside, the Zoo kids acted up inside. No great theory there. Cause and effect. Resentment equaled anger. Retribution equaled revenge. And revenge equaled a white-hot melting pot of adolescent jealousy. That's exactly the behavior that got them there in the first place and, most definitely, the behavior that kept them in the Zoo.

However, to my surprise, in a few weeks, cooperation within the Zoo was increasing, and my trips up to the third floor were few and far between. So with the money, after we got permission from the principal and parents, we arranged a Zoo cookout. Those kids redefined gluttony. They ate fast, very fast, like wolves devouring their prey before bigger wolves took it from them. We even had a fight, a push-and-shove, over a hotdog bun. Ice cream was a bad idea. Soda cans with pop tops were a bad idea. Clean-up was a nightmare.

Cooperation was nonexistent. But kids are kids. After all, the Zoo needed to keep its reputation intact. No worries there.

છ૭૯૭

Aftermath of slutty pirate caper and two days after the semi-formal, on Monday morning:

The door to my office was never locked and was for the most part always open. When I was behind my desk I tried to remain reserved, steely-eyed, and open-mined. I was Switzerland. Because of my neutral stance, students would appear out-of-the-blue in need of many things.

Shortly after the slutty pirate adventure, I was seemingly overrun by girls, alone or in small groups, who had different opinions and different takes on the episode. And usually they wanted to gossip, start rumors, and wreak havoc. And, of course, they wanted me to take sides—their side. I would have been insane to get in the middle of teenage wolf packs or she-wolves stalking each other.

It was fascinating to watch tiny teenage girls, soft-spoken for the most part, turn into raving monsters, spewing insults and trash talk: talk laced with a pinch of hate and jealously. The green-eyed monsters were loose in my office, once again, invading my quiet time and bombarding my eardrums.

These were not women scorned. Oh no, they were upset that the cheerleaders-turned-slutty-pirates, members of the popular clique, the A-Team got off so easy.

"Why did you help them, Officer Hobson? It's not fair. Everyone caters to those losers."

I usually remained mute, slowly shaking my head, and shrugging my shoulders while tapping my pen on my desk as I tapped my feet underneath.

It was a seemingly magical event when the popular cliques were knocked down a few pegs. No joy in Mud-Ville today.

But these green-eyed girls weren't ready to roll over quite yet and, with them in that state of hateful, jealous rage, I learned a few new things and added a few new words to my urban dictionary of high school angst.

"You know the cheerleaders, right, well they are nothing but attention whores," said Danielle, a tenth-grade student and a field hockey player—I think.

And from the cheap seats, "Ya, they're both wicked Barbie bitches who will do anything to get attention—like paint their faces like clowns, push up their bon-bons, make out with your boyfriend like cheat-tang snakes, squirm into your friendships, and fuck up your life. Fuck them, you know what I mean, Jack?" said, Deb, a junior, sighing after her long-winded rant.

"What are bon-bons?" I asked with a furrowed brow.

"Come on, Jack, they're tits!" chimed a little monster, standing in the corner of the office.

"Oh, right, of course. I knew that," I said.

And, not to be silenced, Sara, a popular kid, nice kid said, "That Rhonda chick, the one crying about the semi-formal, she's a Barbie Whore. Want to see her Facebook posts from the semi-formal? They're so lame."

"Not really, no, and don't all of you have better things to do?"

"No, we're supposed to be in the library, but if we say we're with you, it's cool. It is cool, right?"

"For now" I said.

Then all of a sudden, like a pack of wolves picking up a faraway scent or bell or sound, the group stood and, in unison, left. "Bye, bye. See ya. Wouldn't want to be ya," they said as they vanished into a sea of kids.

"Good talk," I said to no one. I looked at my watch. It was 10:30, first lunch.

CHAPTER 6

Nathan: Part of the Landscape

One kid who didn't participate in that school celebration was Nathan, and I knew the reason why.

Earlier in my law enforcement career, I'd learned about gypsies, specifically ones from Eastern Europe. They called themselves Travelers. We knew them as Romany Gypsies, or just "Roms" for short. They called the police muckers or yags, Romanian slang for soldier. As a patrolman, I quickly learned how they would prey on the elderly. One of their favorite scams was to pull up to an established home in a small pickup, some concrete already mixed in its bed, and hopefully find a senior at home.

"You have some holes in your driveway, and we have some extra hot patch," they'd say. "We can start repairing them today and finish the job tomorrow."

All they needed was a five hundred dollar cash deposit. They'd start the job, promise to return, then split, leaving shoddy work behind. Working in pairs, they were some of the best con-men I'd run up against.

Another ploy they tried was knocking on doors, telling the resident that their truck had broken down.

"Could I use your phone to call our boss, have him send out a tow truck?" Then, if encouraged at all, they'd throw in an extra plea, hoping to commit a bit of quick burglary while being aided. "Okay if my partner uses the bathroom?"

Expert thieves, Roms knew where and how to fence their stolen goods and how to pass off trash as a rare find. They could convince a buyer of the damnedest things. A chair from a junkyard, after they fixed it up a little, could become an expensive heirloom.

"This chair," they'd remark about an item that might yield them a profit. "It's a family antique from Eastern Europe."

Roms followed the weather, picking cranberries before the snow and helping to launch carnivals and festivals in the spring. Hard workers by nature, they managed to take care of their families by any means necessary. As for their involvement in wrongdoing, it seemed their criminal activity was limited only by their imaginations.

Now that my beat had changed from the street to the school, I had reason to remember the Roms. I'd been getting reports about an undersized, sophomore, transfer student named Nathan. Fair-skinned and blond, he kept getting into fights and ditching classes. Truant officers were puzzled at how to nail him down. Records proved to be useless in finding the home he'd come from, and he was an expert in eluding any chase outside the school.

Early one morning, the administrative office decided to hold a disciplinary hearing for him and they asked me to attend. Entering the austere office, I acknowledged Nathan with a nod. The kid looked glum, like he'd give anything to be anywhere but there.

The principal introduced me to Nathan's grandfather. "Jack, meet Mr. Johnson."

I put out a hand. "Nice to meet you, sir."

The grandfather shook my hand, under obvious duress, and repeated the question that came from the lips of every parent of a kid in trouble when they were introduced to me, the guy in uniform. "What's the police doing here?"

His voice had a familiar ring, reminding me of Gaelic, and reminiscent of the way the Gypsy dialect could vary from clan to clan. Here was this fellow, ten years older now, who'd once called me a *yag*, his clan's term for cop. At the time I'd thought he'd called me a fag. I remembered that I'd told him to label me anything he wanted to, that I was there to arrest him.

I smiled at him now. Hell, I'd once picked up this old boy for the "fix your driveway" scam. No way was he this kid's grandfather. He was most likely the Gypsy king now, a title earned through attrition.

The principal stepped in. "Jack is here to look out for the kids," he said. "If anything goes badly for them, he'll quell the crisis."

Mr. Johnson scrunched up his face but, for the moment, seemed to be all right with that.

After a brief discussion, it was decided that Nathan would be allowed back into school. There was to be no more fighting or truancy. And to my surprise, Mr. Johnson even agreed to Nathan reporting to the Zoo. The meeting broke up, and Nathan, head down, began his journey upstairs. I made sure I walked outside with Mr. Johnson.

The tension between us was almost palpable.

"Walter," I said. "I haven't seen you for what ten years. Where have you been?"

"What's it to you?" he said, corralling me with a dark look. "What's your problem?"

"I don't have a problem," I said. "I'm not on patrol like the old days. I care about Nathan's education."

"I don't need you around my kid."

"He's not your kid."

"They're all my kids."

I knew he meant his entire clan, including the children, were his responsibility. He hadn't changed. I handed him one of my business cards.

He bristled. "What's this for?"

"Walter, this isn't about you or me. It's about Nathan. If he needs anything, call me."

Without a word, he turned on a heel and left me standing near the school's main gate.

One afternoon in the cafeteria, Nathan got into a food fight with some other goof-offs. Depending on who was supervising the cafeteria, a rift could amount to a national emergency or just another lunch period. This time the teacher on duty was treating the incident with screams and cattle calls. By chance, I'd witnessed enough of the action to wonder why she was taking names and sending kids to the assistant principal.

I decided to sit in with the assistant principal when the band of kids had all drifted into his office. "This is bullshit," I told him privately. "I was there. She's overreacting. Nothing really happened."

He gave the kids an hour of detention.

I handed Nathan and another kid one of my *Knucklehead* notes, little reminders that being stupid wasn't cool.

Everyone went back to class. The next day Nathan didn't show up at school. Days passed, and a truant officer was sent after him. As I suspected, the officer couldn't find his address, and she asked me to join the search. This was old New England, where townships overlapped. Streets ended and started up again when you least expected them to. Finally, with the truant officer aboard, I pulled my vehicle into a place called Peter's Pond, where camping was allowed. The pond was good-sized, and surrounded by several RVs, many of them state-of-the-art units.

"We've found the camp," I told the truant officer.

"I don't want to deal with them."

"They're just people," I said.

I preferred confronting parents where they lived. They usually talked more freely in their own comfort zones. Often they'd surprise me and ask me into their homes. And I make it a point to remember that I was a guest. I'd found that even the toughest parents can be afraid of what is happening with their own kids and wish to examine, along with me, the threatening divide between them and their teen-aged children.

After we parked, I got out of the car alone and came across a middle-aged guy who seemed to be governing the compound.

I showed him my cop smile. "Who are you?"

"None of your business, yag."

"I want to see some identification," I said. "And I'm not going to ask you a second time."

He opened his wallet and took out a Virginia driver's license. I looked it over, knowing the odds were good that he hadn't gotten it from the Virginia DMV.

"Lawrence, nice name. What's your middle initial and your date of birth?" I asked as my eyes darted from the license picture to his face and back. Obtaining a fake driving license is child's play these days. "Same last name as Walter. You two related?"

No response.

"Okay, Larry. I'm coming back about 2:30," I said. "Tell Walter I need to talk to him."

After school, I went back to the camp. Walter was there, sitting at a table talking to a bunch of other people. He shot me a nasty glance.

"I told you I don't want to deal with any yags," he said. "We've decided to home school Nathan."

I nodded a useless greeting to his constituency. "It doesn't work that way."

The old man pulled a piece of paper from his shirt pocket. "Did you give this to the boy?" He was waving my *Knucklehead* notice in the air. "What the hell does it mean?"

"It means that Nathan hasn't reached the point of any real trouble," I said. "The note is my way of telling him to wise up before he gets there."

The group at the table collectively looked toward the RVs, where a woman was heading our way. Then I saw Nathan had joined her. *Mother and son*, I thought, *no doubt coming my way reluctantly.*

"Nathan," I said. "How you doing?"

He didn't say anything, but I could tell he was satisfied with his surroundings, maybe downright happy. And when you came right down to it, that was good enough for me.

Holding Nathan's hand, his mother strolled up to me. "I was going to call the school," she said. "We took care of the problem here."

"There's a process if you want to take your kid out of school," I told her. "Just having him disappear shoots up a lot of red flags." I paused to get the entire group's attention. "The school begins to worry and sends out a truant officer. You need to call the school, go through the guidance counselor, and get all of Nathan's records."

Walter jumped in. "We're taking him out of public school because it's drawing too much attention to us," he said. "Gypsies already have a bad name."

Such an admission caught me off balance. "You're overreacting," I said. "It's like calling an Irish person a mick. We all go through that if you think about it. But you can't paint all ethnic groups with a dirty brush."

Walter scowled. "I told you I don't want to deal with a yag."

"You trying to hurt my feelings, Walter?" I kidded.

No smile, just a soft under-the-breath, "Fuck off."

"That's not particularly endearing either, Walter," I said, then I addressed the mother. "You said you took care of this. What do you mean?"

Walter spoke before she could answer. "Our women have a strong influence over people, especially kids. They take care of them in their own way."

"What does that mean?"

Now the mother stepped forward. "For the last three nights, I've been praying over him."

"Who are you praying to?"

"It's not like what you think."

"What's it like?"

"When a child is doing something that brings attention to us," she said, "when he ends up having to defend his honor among the other children and that brings the soldiers into the picture—"

"Maybe I can better understand if you elaborate."

"I place a lock of my hair next to my child for three nights," she said.

I'd learned years ago something about this practice which involved a carefully braided lock of the mother's hair preserved for such evocations. "And?"

Nathan's mother seemed reluctant to go on.

Walter cleared his throat. "Gypsy mothers have a strong influence over their children." He looked about, as if waiting for the others' attention. "When it was time, we asked Nathan to rise from his bed. We sat down next to him and told him the story of Opel."

Sounded familiar, a proverb of sorts, but I needed more information. "Opel?"

"From the old country," Walter said. "Opel disobeyed the camp's rules."

This was new to me. "Is this some kind of myth?"

"No more than the stories you tell your kids." He allowed me a minute to absorb that. "Opel brought outsiders to the Gypsy camp, bad men who enslaved and, in some cases, killed members of Opel's family. Many of our people were forced to run as outlaws."

"And that's why you became Travelers?" I was careful not to refer to the outcasts as Roms or even nomads.

"That's why," Walter said, "we are constantly trying to rebuild our culture."

I was still thinking about Nathan, the way he was standing near his mother, a seemingly unbreakable bond. "So what else made you feel it would work out better to keep Nathan here rather than trust our classrooms?"

"There's a chant that the mother says," Walter said.

"Papa—" Nathan's mother said, "—don't tell him that."

"It's okay," he said.

The woman set her eyes on me. It was plain she was a true believer in what she had decided was best for her son. "It's about what Opel did and about whether it is possible to do again." She hesitated briefly, then her words broke the silence. "But with a single change of name, the story fits you quite the same."

I was fascinated. She had brought the myth of Opel full circle, back to Nathan's relationship with the entire clan. *Hell*, I thought, *we* have *lost him*.

We had a conversation about people raising kids and we talked more about religion. We talked about faith and how important it was to keep faith alive. All of a sudden, I realized that this conversation, between cop and Gypsy king on his home turf, was exceptional, an eclipse of an event, rare and powerful. We were just two men, equals bullshitting about life.

I understood all at once what I had suspected all along: that Gypsies are a paradox, a cultural phenomenon. Their life blood is the family, and everything they do is for the collective good of the family. And I realized that Nathan's public school experience was an experiment, or at least an attempt to expose him to white kids his own age, to experience the academic freedoms of the middle class. But it came down to the fact that Gypsies are better off with their people—their mothers and all their surrogate fathers and tutors and role models so important for growth into the Romany life style. It is the bond that ties them to their heritage and forwards their traditions. They exist on the fringe of society, alongside it, but never crossing over that very well-defined cultural line. Once a Gypsy always a Gypsy. If you left the clan, you were gone for good. There was no coming back. Nathan didn't have time to choose. That decision was made for him. His exposure to my high school had lasted a turbulent sixteen days.

But I had many other questions that went unanswered, like how could they reconcile their criminal enterprises—their life of crime and schemes and scams—while still holding on tight to their ultra conservative Christian beliefs. To them, it wasn't a life of crime. It was what they did to take care of the clan, and it was what generations past had done on three continents for more than 2000 years.

Although I was outnumbered five to one, I felt no animosity—at the moment anyway. That fact that he would allow me in and talk with me was something I'd never believed possible.

"White people are a plague to the Gypsy community," said the old king. "And their rules, laws, and racial tolerance is like a virus that weakens our bonds," he said with conviction. I took that to mean that they were intolerant people, but I guess cops are a necessary evil to them. Always around, always looking for them.

In retrospect, two things surprised me. One was that I was let into their camp, and two, that I was, to some extent, allowed inside the king's head. His thoughtful questions, and answers to mine, proved that to me. Other than my brief interaction with Nathan's mom, no one else spoke, but they stood their ground like sentinels and watched my every move like a spider watches a fly caught in his web. But there I was, alone, keeping eye contact with the king and engaging in a debate about life, the love of a mother, and the importance of a family—no different than my beliefs about all I hold dear and what I'm thankful for in my life.

After an hour, I asked him, "Do you still have my business card?"

"No."

"I figured as much."

I gave him another one. "I'll make a deal with you. If you put Nathan back in school, and he gets into any trouble, I'll see to it that I handle it. That way he won't have to hassle with the principal." I was trying to barter Nathan's return to school with a promise that I would protect him and that ultimately any decision made about Nathan would be Walter's.

I was thinking about the theory of cultural transformation, cultural resilience, and generational influence. I knew that, stuck in his own culture, a kid like Nathan had limited options. There were no helpful studies that dealt with the Rom-Gypsy sect and the formal education of their children. Being wanderers, they expected, when a place seemed right, to set up a long-term camp, run their scams, and enroll in public schools. But it's a fragile and delicate existence. It takes very little to spook them back to the road. They are suspicious and superstitious folk.

Kids, when exposed to other kids with similar experiences, more often than not don't expand their choices. And the rub, if they never leave their small, cult-like communities they become absorbed in the culture and become part of the landscape outside of school. I didn't want that to happen to Nathan.

The old king took my card and slapped the table in a gesture that I understood to mean it was time for me to go.

The next morning, I sat down with Nathan's guidance counselor. "There's a chance we might get Nathan back today," I told him.

After first period was well under way, the truant officer on the case came in. "Nathan isn't here today," she reported.

All of a sudden, I felt twenty years older. "Did his mother call in, say he was sick?"

"No."

"We'll give it a day."

The following day, I had the same conversation with the truant officer. Nathan was still a no show.

"Want to take a ride?" I asked her.

"We're going back there?"

"Yeah."

We went to the camp. That's all it was—a camp, no evidence of Nathan's family. No RVs in sight, not a trace of the Gypsies. Everybody had vanished.

I had run a lot of license plates and had passed the information to my guys on patrol. BOLO was the acronym we used: "Be On the Look Out for these license numbers." Since the Roms, in this case, had committed no crimes that I was aware of, I didn't notify the other towns. It was still sunny, and enough carnivals were breaking ground that they could do day work for pay. They could hide in plain sight.

I still wonder about Nathan. He's older now. Maybe pulling a pickup, with rosary beads hanging from the rearview, up in front of someone's house, the Gypsy king next to him, pointing out how the old driveway scam might be perfect right there. He'd be wearing his coming-of-age ring, good for show but better for fights. But he'd be a Gypsy, through and through.

I had figured it would be good for Nathan to interact with other students and to be part of something more than what he'd been born into. And I was naïve, thinking I had all of the answers.

I never saw him again.

CHAPTER 7

Girl Fights: Emotional Black Eyes

Tragedy, to my students, was in the eye of the beholder. I considered what happened with Nathan, the Gypsy kid, a tragedy.

Fights in high school are common. I'd take Las Vegas odds that there was a fight every day. At lunchtime, with two hundred kids in the cafeteria at any one time, and the frenzy that goes along with that, there's going to be trouble. Girls fought with hands, teeth, and feet. They were more primal. Boys went for the dropped-palms approach—fists up, and it was on. In larger cities and bigger school districts, brass knuckles, little box cutters, Swiss Army knives, and even filed-down toothbrushes were commonplace, according to what I heard from my counterparts.

When fights were bad, the school called the involved students' parents. With boys, it was usually their mothers who raised hell after being called. With girls, it was their fathers. But parents rarely raised hell with their kids. They were mad at the school, or at the other kid involved, or even at the other kid's parents.

It was easy to spot a fight brewing. Two girls might start ragging on each other, maybe two sets of girls, or perhaps two different cliques. And the threats would continue for the rest of the school day. Most of the events involved boy trouble, and the battle lines would be drawn.

Usually, the two girls who fought would be sent home and suspended for a few days, and we would have to watch for followers who might want to continue the battle. But follow ups and rematches were rare. Second offenses meant possible charges filed against them by me. Usually, a call to the culprits' parents would end the war between second offenders. If not, I'd step in and threaten to file charges against them.

Away from school, fights would break out at parties, or at the mall, or wherever students hung out. When reports of trouble came in to me, I'd usually get boys shaking hands in a couple of days. Girls tended to hold grudges forever. Even if there was a rumor, that was enough to get the fists flying. They would spread hate clubs, and whole groups of girls would bombard a hapless opponent with threats.

On one particular Monday, when all of the problems from the weekend seemed to snowball during a lunch period, two senior girls started a ruckus. These were nice girls, good students who usually stayed clear of my radar. Yet today, as their voices ascended in volume, I got that weird feeling that usually preceded an outbreak.

The teacher on duty feared the worst. "Jack," she warned me, "they're going to fight."

The school had a different sound when things were happening, especially when a fight was beginning to develop. The tone wasn't the only thing that changed. Kids gravitated toward where the fight was going to happen and formed a boxing ring around the two scrappers. I'd push my way in to where the girls were fighting. Everyone would back off when they saw me, but the cat calling and heckling would go on.

Boys, deep down, wanted the fight broken up. Girls jumped rapidly into kill mode, where controlling them could be a dangerous task. Fighters would use this time to take a quick breather before going at it again. I'd learned to be a referee, by putting myself between them. Many times as a roadblock, I'd get punched and scratched.

Most of my injuries took place after the contenders hit the ground. While in such a frenzy, the words *police* or *cop* or *stop* meant little to them. These girls would kick, bite, and pull hair on the ground. Kids would get kicked with a boot in the cheekbone, and I'd take my share of kicks and blows as well. I got hit below the belt a few times, like maybe knocking the wind out of me was the intended goal of the battler.

And everything happened fast in these rough engagements. In an instant, punches were thrown, hair was pulled, the combatants locked together as one, rolling on the floor, flopping like fish out of water, all asses and elbows. The male teachers usually wouldn't break up fights involving female students. Grabbing inappropriately lurked on everybody's minds. I, on the other hand, would grab whatever I could grab to get them apart. As a former hockey referee, I separate people by using the most efficient force, always short of causing injury.

Once in a while, a fight would break out without warning or reason. I happened to witness a real brawl that happened in the hallway fairly close to the cafeteria. Two girls were going at it big time before we knew it. Witnesses chipped in their hoots and cat calls.

"Kill her, bite her, get her," a fight fan shouted.

Others picked up the chant. They weren't necessarily taking sides. They just wanted to see a fight.

I saw blood on the floor. And hair, which was common. A teacher and I broke them up. I could see blood had spilled but couldn't readily find where it was coming from. Both girls were out of breath, and it took a few minutes for the adrenaline to run down. Fights had individual results as far as injuries went. No fight seemed to leave a predictable result.

The assistant principal, Nick, and I finally separated the girls and, after deciding neither was badly wounded, took them to the nurse's office. They, of course, showed signs of being in a wrestling match, both of them bleeding from scratches. When Maria, the nurse, found that one girl was still bleeding, she began to treat her. The assessment was quick. This girl had just suffered a hair pulling that involved her hair extensions.

"They're very well connected—" Maria told us, "—to the hair that, in turn, was connected to the scalp."

I looked at Nick. "We learn something new every day."

When the mother came in and realized what had happened, she immediately focused on money as opposed to her daughter's physical injuries. She offered no, "Honey, are you okay?" Instead the first words out of her mouth went something like: "Those hair extensions cost me two hundred dollars."

I again gave Nick a glance. "Every day, something new."

The mother was mad there had been a fight, but she also wanted me to charge the other girl with assault and battery because of the extensions.

I told her what I told most parents in her situation. "I have no problem filing charges, but if I do, I'm charging both of them equally."

"But my daughter is the one who had her extensions ruined."

"If you can prove the fight was over the hair extensions, and the opposing girl fought only to pull the hair extensions out, then okay," I said. "But hair pulling is hair pulling. It doesn't matter if it's that or a punch to the face. If these charges are going forward, they're going forward, and it will be both girls."

The two girls didn't like each other to begin with, probably because they were friends with other girls who didn't like each other, something that is timeless. We all can remember this peer behavior from our own school days.

The irate mother's view of the fight happened to be more monetary. She wasn't focused on her daughter's bad behavior. "I'll go over your head," she barked at me. "The police chief is a friend of mine."

"I'll give you his telephone number," I said as I'd done many times to parents, in similar situations, who suddenly decided they were on a first-name basis with the chief. "Do what you have to do. I'm not arresting anybody."

❧❧❧

Another day early in the school year, I was doing my usual walk about, checking doors and locks, and breaking up small groups of aimlessly wandering kids, when Maria called me from her office.

"Two girls got in a fight," she said. "We have them both here. One of the girls had her front tooth knocked out."

Most of the slap-and-grab fights were directed straight to the principal, but Maria thought I had better look at this one first.

"We have to call both fighters' parents," I told her.

Jillian was a pretty girl, and she had lost one of her front teeth. Briana, the other girl, had broken it off at the root, and she had a cut on her knuckle from where her hand had struck Jillian's mouth. It was traumatic and both girls were in tears. Jillian was a senior and something like this on her record could affect her future college education.

Maria gave both of them ice bags and put Briana in a separate room.

We had Jillian's emergency number for her mother, but we couldn't reach her. On the advice of the nurse, her parents needed to take her to an emergency room for the loss of her tooth. The only person we could get was the stepdad and Jillian didn't want him to be involved.

"He'll go ballistic," she said. "Don't call my stepfather. I don't want him here."

"That may be, but I'm calling him," I said.

Jillian's stepfather was a piece of work, and my first impression when he answered the phone was that he was already pissed off about something. "Is this Jillian's dad," I asked.

He returned my question with, "Who the fuck is this?"

"This is the police officer at the high school— Officer Hobson." I said as calmly as I could.

Instead of asking about Jillian, he ratcheted up his already angry tone with obscenities that fired out of his mouth with each breath. It was an increasingly colorful tirade. Before I could get a word in edgewise and tell him about the fight and Jillian's new dental problem, he yelled, "I'll be right there."

And, with that, the line when dead with a bang. Everyone was in a hyped-up mode. The kids perceived fights as entertainment. As long as they weren't involved, they loved it. For the next few moments, things were traumatic.

Briana's mother came in upset that her daughter might have a scar on her knuckle.

"Have your doctor look at it," I said. "See what you need to do. But I want to talk to you before you leave."

Jillian's irate dad was soon to be an irate visitor, but I was prepared for that contingency. A short time later, about thirty-five minutes, Stepdad lived up to his charming personality by storming through the front door. Didn't sign in. Didn't show any identification. Didn't follow procedure or protocol. Threatened everyone he perceived as staff. I rushed out to where the commotion was and waved off the people in the main office. Before I took him back to see his stepdaughter, we went into a vacant office. I told him very clearly to calm down, and if he didn't he'd be leaving and I'd wait for his wife before releasing Jillian. Steaming but stoically quiet, I brought him to Jillian.

She was crying, and I got a very strong feeling it had more to do with her fear of her stepdad than the loss of her tooth.

I introduced him to Maria and myself as Jack. The mad dad was Mike. "Where's the other girl?" he demanded.

"Let's not go there right now," I said. "Let's talk about your daughter. There was a fight. She was involved, and she's going to be suspended."

"I want to file charges," he said, without even knowing the facts of what had happened.

I walked away from him calmly and phoned for backup. "We have an unwanted guest," I said into the phone. "A disturbance caused by a parent, and I have a feeling I might need some help."

My team downtown knew I never called unless it was serious, and I expected them to respond quickly.

"Briana's mother wants to talk to you," Maria said. "She wants to take the girl out of school right now."

"Is that the other girl?" the stepfather asked. Then like a crazy person, he went toward the room where we'd separated Briana's knuckle from Jillian's lost tooth.

He probably would have grabbed her, but I didn't let it go that far.

"I'm going to take care of you," he said to the mother. "I know where you live."

"Calm down, Mike, you're in a public high school," I said, tensing a bit myself. "Watch your language or we'll take this outside or down to the police station."

He was really hostile, bordering on maniacal. In some way, he thought the mother was responsible for the fight. His anger was directed at her. Not choosing to verbally attack me, the principal, or the nurse, he rushed right into where Briana was with her mother—going in like a linebacker, screaming that he was going to sue her. It was immediately clear to me that we were dealing with a rage-fueled bully with no common sense and primal social skills.

"Great, why are they always two feet taller than me?" I said out loud to nobody in particular.

"My daughter was thinking of a modeling career. Now what is she going to do? You've ruined her life." He was about six-foot-four and, at the moment, crazed.

As he tried to get past me and *to* her, he grabbed me by my shirt. The pupils of his eyes looked dilated to me. Drugs, I thought. And his inappropriate response to a school fight was too over-the-top. I looked at him very calmly, one hand on my pepper spray. I really wanted to mace this asshole, but using pepper spray in an enclosed space meant everyone got hit. The burning effects spread indiscriminately and that would be bad, really bad. I had another option of control if Mike's rage increased. As a part of my gun belt, I carried a tactical baton called an Asp—like a snake. It's a truncheon, an innocent-looking, rubber-enclosed baton. If I snapped it out with one motion, the rubber would become a handle, and it would open up to twenty-one inches of hard steel. When a cop is out on the street, it's totally different. I was in a school, and I had to show some restraint. And our audience was getting exponentially bigger—insects to a light.

"Make a really good decision right now," I told him, "because if you go through me again, it's not going to end well for you."

"What are you going to do? What are you, a security guard?" he taunted, still wicked pissed off.

"What are you, totally out of your fucking mind, right now?" I countered. "What do you want me to do, Mike? You assaulted a police officer, and if I were you I'd back off, because you are about to be seriously outnumbered. And I suspect you won't be leaving the building under your own power. So you make a decision. How is this fiasco going to end?"

Enter Big Nick and a science teacher named Kevin. Kevin stood about six-foot-three and was about equal in size to the crazy dad. And Big Nick was a head taller than both.

The color of Mike's face changed from red to crimson with each breath. I could see his body tensing. His eyes darted around the room as if looking for the path of least resistance. He was working himself into a rage.

He moved forward and tried to push me out of his way so he could face the mother. I grabbed him and held on. We were locked up in a kind of bizarre dance. He was trying to shake me off, I was looking him directly in his eyes, commanding, yelling for him to stop, to relax, and to calm down.

He was very strong and getting stronger. Adrenaline will do that.

We're trained to stay right inside someone's box, someone's personal space—crowd them. That way they can't take a full swing. So I held on tight, trying to counter his strength and keep him off balance.

Big Nick and Kevin each grabbed an arm and, without restraint or hesitation, pulled the dad off me. The struggle continued to the floor.

And then, all at once, the room was full of police officers. They were younger than Mike, stronger, and obviously pissed off that he was shaking me like a rag doll. The dad's overinflated ego deflated. Immediately, the lion turned into a lamb.

We needed him out of the building, either pleasantly escorted out of the school or dragged outside in handcuffs. He calmed down a bit, but nevertheless, he was roughly dragged out of the room like a kid dragging an empty refrigerator box. Subsequently, he was arrested, charged with assault and battery on a police officer and disturbing the peace. He was never allowed back on school property. Jillian refused to leave with her stepdad. We arranged for an ambulance for her.

Briana's mother wanted to press charges on Jillian's father. "If anybody is going to press charges on him, it's going to be me," I said. "You don't worry about that. If I charge him with assault and battery on a police officer, it's going to be much worse for him."

That calmed her down. Charges would be pending, and I knew that tempers would fade as timed passed. But paperwork was filed, keeping Jillian's stepfather off school property.

Both girls were suspended.

"I'm a senior," Jillian said to me. "I can't have this on my record."

"It won't be on your record," I told her. "I'll take care of it."

She was grateful for that and happy that I didn't hurt her stepdad. Her mother came in later. "I'm so sorry I wasn't available," she said, no doubt realizing her husband had been out of line.

As time went by, and Jillian's tooth was fixed, her stepfather was still worried I was going to do something. He was a different person when I talked to him the second time.

Jillian had already been accepted to college and didn't want to push it. "My parents want to press charges and sue these people, but I'm graduating. I don't want any trouble."

"You're eighteen years old," I told her. "You make the decision. You don't have to do it."

The two girls agreed to accept a mutual understanding. After a couple of weeks of being pissed off and threatening to go over my head, their parents calmed down.

Those fights at school gave me insight to the dynamics of the families involved. Parents don't always grow with their kids as much as they should. When their kids get into trouble, the parents see them as they were in middle and elementary school.

These kids got themselves into trouble, but the parents wouldn't let them get themselves out of trouble. The parents wanted to come in and make a stand for them, sometimes very inappropriately. A lot of parents don't realize the forum they're in when they lose control of themselves. I always wondered what they were like at home, where there were no filters.

When Jillian returned to school after her suspension, she came into my office for advice and to vent a little.

"I've been arguing with my stepdad since the fight," she told me. "He's so unreasonable about my problems in and out of school."

"In what way?"

Her face changed. "I'm your father," she said in an exaggerated voice, mimicking the guy who'd given us such a bad time about the fight when he'd barged in knowing nothing about the facts. "I'll fight your battles. I'll protect you. You'll always be my little girl. Rebellion is childish."

"You got him down," I said, trying to hide my grin. "Not bad, not bad at all."

She continued in a more serious tone. "He's overly protective and worries that I'll be taken advantage of."

"By whom?" I asked.

"'Everyone and anyone,' he says." Then with tears rolling down her cheeks and with a hiccup, she asked me in her own voice, "Why won't he let me grow up? How can I convince him to lighten up and let me have more control over my life?"

I thought about her dilemma. I'd heard it before. "Can I offer a word of advice?" I asked her. "It's cheap."

She smiled.

"Good, a smile will dry your eyes," I said. "Your stepfather means well, but he's an opposing character, and his bark is loud. Please correct me if I'm wrong or out of line, but I would call him a rescue parent. One who rescues you from everything, out of guilt, fear, worry, and a thousand different reasons unique to your relationship with him."

Too many words, I thought, *and too much surmising on my part.*

But she seemed to be mulling what I'd said over in her mind. She needed to take charge of her own life. She would soon be among university students, most of whom wouldn't try knocking her tooth out in a million years.

"Jillian," I said, "teenagers make mistakes, and it is hoped that with each mishap, a lesson is learned. But not every teenager gets the opportunity to learn from their mistakes. Those who have rescue parents may be shielded from important lessons well into adulthood."

"Well," she said, "I had one big lesson." She gave me a look as if she'd just aged a couple of years.

"What, Jillian?"

"The fight was over a boy I probably won't ever really care about anymore."

"But your dad interfered," I said. "He wanted to fix everything, because in his mind, you can do no wrong."

There was a lesson to be learned. I wanted so to help her, but how do you cover all the mistakes you've made yourself?

I told her she'd broken a few rules and that, when we do that, we should try everything in our power not to repeat our mistakes. But now she was on her own.

"When parents rescue their kids from challenges, they send a message to them that they are fragile, lacking in skills, and incapable of overcoming obstacles that other kids are able to surmount." I mentioned how codependency could create monsters. "You want to be independent, treated like a mature young lady, right?"

Like most of the youths I've talked to, she remained silent after my sermon. Until she repeated the most common answer, one she'd never admit to months, even days before.

"Right," she admitted.

"But don't fight any more battles in my hallways, okay?"

"Thanks, Officer Hobson," she said.

"It's all good, my friend," I told her, like it was a sure bet. At least it was even odds.

CHAPTER 8

Murphy: The Fight Club

Girls had their way of fighting, and so did boys. Think back to your school days. Do you remember the middle school boy whose reputation preceded him? He was the one who shaved first and had a car. A car in middle school—every school system has had its share of such kids. They drift through the halls and classes, egotistically cool and aloof, maintaining their status as the alpha male.

Murphy was a boy like that. Older than other students in his classes, he'd been held back a year or more for reasons not clearly explained on his transcripts. Alerted to his notoriety, I decided to pay him a visit the summer before his sophomore year. I thought meeting him on his own turf might prepare me for his upcoming transition to high school. We called these visits proactive community-policing. Since I was the juvenile officer, I thought I'd make first contact, a pre-emptive meeting, a friendly meet and greet. He was out on the street, skateboarding with other neighborhood kids, so I rolled up and spoke to them. We talked about summer and school in the fall. I was talking to them collectively, trying not to single out Murphy, but I did get a feel for him and we made eye contact.

He lived in what we called a nice neighborhood—the kind of section that I'd learned could produce as many troubled teens as any other.

I knew of Murphy's family from my days as a patrol officer but, at the time, I had not yet met young Murphy, although I was aware of him.

One night, one of Murphy's sister's called 911. His mother and father were in the midst of a brawl when I got there. Dad was drunk again, aggressive, and mean. At any moment, he could attack anyone. We arrested him. That was the first time I had been in their house. Murphy was in the kitchen, standing guard over his mom. He didn't say anything. It was no secret that his dad had beaten Mom up a few times. Murphy was seventeen. I suspected he'd been drinking as well, but I didn't go there. His father's behavior, for the time being, had made everybody else in the family look straight as an arrow.

Within the context of domestic violence, it's important for police officers to assess the home environment and to look for the silent victims, the children. We would find them hiding under beds, in closets, squirreling themselves away from the fighting and away from the sounds that often preceded violent family events.

That September, Murphy entered high school as a sophomore. Six-feet tall and sporting a black beard, he appeared villainous. Grunge clothing, mostly second-hand military stuff, covered his wiry frame. The olive drab sweater and fatigue jacket looked like they'd been pulled out of Goodwill boxes.

Big Nick, the school's assistant principal, was a forty-year veteran of the school system. His nickname was a well-deserved handle, and he had been through good and bad times with scores of kids like Murphy. A former semi-pro football player, Nick could be explosive when it came to disciplining kids, but he was also devoted to their general wellbeing. He was a wonderful mentor. If a kid needed discipline, members of the faculty would take him to see Nick for what he termed a *tune up*.

I often saw Nick with Murphy, but the oversized assistant principal never called me about him. Then one morning, I got the word he wanted me to stop by his office.

"Jack," he said, before I could grab a seat, "I need a favor."

"Anything for you," I said. "Up to a point, of course."

"Of course." The small chuckle in his great chest flattened into a sigh. "I got Murphy into a detox center for teenagers," he said. "It's a self-commit place, and he's going to be gone for ninety days. I like this kid, Jack, and I'm going to try and save him. I need to shuttle his assignments back and forth to the Castle."

The Castle had a real name. The Clean And Sober Teens Living Empowered was a renovated pump station that housed up to twenty-four teenage patients. The old building, with its parapets and landscape of obsolete railroad tracks, sat on a hill just outside of Brockton.

I told Nick that I thought he'd made a good choice. "It might be just the program for Murphy," I said.

Nick knew I was frequently in that area of town visiting my mother. "Would you stop by once in a while," he asked, "just to see how Murph's doing?"

"Yeah, I can do that."

The next day, and many following it, I drove out to the Castle. Without going past the office, I would leave homework assignments and other school correspondence for Murphy. Sometimes I'd check out his homework and help organize it before I turned it in. He had no idea I was the one who picked up and delivered his assignments.

After a few months, he returned to school. That was about the time the fights started breaking out.

Unlike the spontaneous confrontations between students I was used to, these battles seemed pre-arranged. They would break out at the end of one second floor hallway, where the only way out was a staircase. The only people who needed to be in *that* hallway were janitors or people carrying out specific tasks. I heard what sounded like a fight brewing on the second floor after one Friday's final bell. This particular hallway ran directly under the gym, but there was no athletic event scheduled.

Schools have different sounds, and I was well attuned to most of them. The noise was different when there was a fight. It was almost like the clamor of fans at a sporting event.

Following the rise and fall of voices, I soon came upon a large cluster of kids. "Hey, what's going on here?" I shouted.

Not a good idea. In a split second, twenty kids turned and ran toward me. I thought I was going to be stampeded. At the end of the charge, a stray kid fell and ended up at my feet.

"Get up," I said. "Let's have a look at you." The kid picked himself up. His lip was bleeding and a bruise on his jaw was growing by the second. I noticed a few of his buddies had hung around, no doubt in a show of support.

"It looks like you took a punch from Rocky," I said.

The kid fingered his chin. "A what, a punch from Rocky Balboa?"

I couldn't help trying to bridge the generation gap with this kid and the few others who'd partaken in what they'd presumed to be a boxing match. "Rocky Marciano, undisputed heavyweight champion of the world, never lost a fight," I repeated. "A fighter from my hometown, Brockton." I let them chew on that. "Now, tell me what happened."

"Nothing," he murmured. "Just a fight."

"What was it about?"

"Stupid stuff."

I told everyone but the injured kid to break it up. "All of you, get out of here now and go home. I don't want to see any of you hanging around the school."

I aided the wounded scrapper down to the nurse's office. There, I got his name and pulled his records while Maria took photos of his injuries. I went over the usual questions with the boy. About how everything had started and what I could do to stop it from happening again. But I knew that I'd eventually have to send him home without getting much out of him. Before he left, I took a photo of his wound with my phone. This was no ordinary fight. Something didn't feel right to me about it.

Jake the Fake was one of my snitches. He would come in and tell me all the rumors in school, things he overheard, things he made up. One of the nurse's chronic hypochondriacs, he used Maria as a sounding board. Between the two of us, we extracted bits of information from him about the school fights occurring like clockwork.

"There's going to be another one today after school," he told me one day in my office. When I quizzed him about it, he replied, "I think they are holding it in the sandpits on the other side of town."

"How are they going to get there?"

"They plan these things out," he said. "They have a regular car pool system."

"Give me one name."

He hesitated.

"A name, Jake," I said. "Now."

"Murphy," he said. "He's the promoter."

Somehow that didn't surprise me.

After school that day, I went straight to the station and told them about the fight that might be happening at the pits. A cruiser was dispatched to the location, but it came back later with no information about a fight taking place.

The next day after I returned from fishing for tardy students on the streets, Maria called.

"Jack, we've got a kid in here who says he fell off a skateboard last night. You need to see him."

First thing I did was check out the patient's elbows.

"No scuff marks," I said. "Let me see your knees."

The kid squirmed. "I landed on my face."

"Ass over tea kettle, right?"

That brought a smile and seemed to break the ice.

I took a photo and left him for Maria to patch up. Maybe I could get something out of him later.

Out in the hall, I met up with Jake the Fake.

"Headed for the nurse?" I asked him. "Hoping to get out of a test today, are you?"

"No," he said sheepishly.

"You were right on the money, Jake," I said in a sarcastic tone that I hoped would get him to tell me what he knew. "So sure there was going to be a fight in the pits."

"It didn't happen in the pits," he said. "It happened at the wall."

The wall was the isolated foundation of a building that had fallen to bad times years ago.

"How do you know this?" I asked. "Were you there?"

He just looked at me and smiled.

I decided to leave it at that. Sometimes you had to settle for what snitches would give you.

Later in the week, I was starting to hear rumblings about the pits. After school on Thursday, I drove down there. All I found were broken bottles, candy wrappers, cigarette butts, all sorts of debris. On Friday, I heard that a big fight was scheduled at the pits. I'd had my fill about the sandpits, the wall, the rampant fighting among students, and the mounting feeling of trouble that permeated the school like a ticking bomb. Then on Sunday morning, one of my sergeants called me.

"They had a big disturbance down at the pits last night," the sergeant said. "A lot of kids got hurt. Do you know anything about it?"

I told him that I'd get back to him. Then I called Nick, the assistant principal, and told him what I had learned about the situation.

"I smell Murphy all over this," I told him. "He's the only one who could pull off a fight club this big."

"I'll have him in my office first thing Monday morning," Nick said. "We'll get to the bottom of this."

"I'll check with you on Monday," I said, not giving him a time. I had a feeling I'd be busy most of the morning.

The next Monday, five minutes after I'd arrived at school, I stood outside the guidance counselor's office. Denny, a kid who always seemed to be on the fringe of many cliques, was waiting for me, along with his parents. Even from the hall, I noticed that Denny's right eye was swollen shut.

The guidance counselor waved me in. "Denny," he instructed the boy, "tell Officer Hobson here what happened to you Saturday night."

Right away, I got a vicious look from Denny's father. I took a deep breath. Over the years I'd learned it was always the parents of kids in trouble who challenged my presence.

"What is he doing here?" the father demanded.

Most parents demand justice, but when justice eyed their kids, they faltered and more often than not, backed off or considered another strategy.

"Why don't we let your son tell us his story," I said. "That way we can start to unravel this whole thing about fighting." I glanced at the guidance counselor. "That is what we're aiming to do here, isn't it?"

Denny looked trapped. He finally mumbled something about being approached by his friends. "They wanted me to get two kids I know to fight each other."

His father jumped in to help him. "Specifically, it was a kid named Murphy," he said. "He's an older kid, running his own fight club." Normally, I'd have stopped him from interrupting, but I felt he wasn't just trying to get his kid off the hook. Maybe he had something to offer. "Denny did get the two kids to agree to a match down at the pits."

I didn't know what the prize was for winning other than status. But for kids in high school who are on the edge, that's like gold.

"It was all arranged," the father went on. "Murphy was the promoter." He gave his son a long look. "Denny has told me how it worked. They use Facebook to draw a crowd."

I'd seen something in the way he'd eyed his son. "But this time it worked differently?"

Denny nodded, but it was his dad who spoke. "Everybody got to the pits. They all formed a circle. Two big boys came up behind Denny and grabbed him." Here the father stopped to control his voice. "And they beat the shit out of him. Kicked him to the ground, called him names. Made him lick their boots."

Okay, I thought, *I'm missing something. Denny's involvement with this fight crowd is not happenstance.*

"Denny, back up, talk to me about your role in this fight game," I probed. "Before you were betrayed and beaten up."

"Well, I thought I was Murphy's friend," Denny said in a low voice. "He even made me his assistant."

I could see his father's eyes grow wide with wonder or confusion or anger. Maybe he thought that Denny had duped him. "You were his *what*? His *assistant*? You mean you helped him *arrange* this bullshit?"

I did a little catching up about Denny in my mind and remembered something. "Denny," I said then waited for him to look at me. "Did you ever have a confrontation with this kid Murphy before he made you his assistant?"

Denny had trouble clearing his throat. "No, never, I thought we were friends," he said.

"Why don't we leave this alone right now? And, Denny, try to put together a timeline for me—serious stuff like dates and times and witnesses. Okay?" I asked, making eye-contact with Dad. "I want to discuss the matter with the assistant principal. Nick told me that he was getting a hold of Murphy this morning." I faced the parents with what I hoped was a concerned smile. "We'll need some photos taken of Denny's facial injuries in the nurse's office. Meanwhile, I'll keep you informed at every level."

The guidance counselor took it from there and I went to see what Nick could tell me about our fight promoter.

Nick still had Murphy in his office when I got there. His office was one of my favorite hangouts. Large, comfortable chairs, dark-stained wooden desk, plenty of file cabinets full of information. Immediately, I chose the chair next to the one holding Murphy and moved into his personal space.

"Murph, do you know Officer Hobson?" Nick asked the kid.

Murphy glanced at me. "Yeah, I've seen him."

"He's the one who brought your homework to the Castle."

Murphy tried to look unimpressed, but I could tell something was registering at some level within him that I had helped him. Normally, I'd advise him of his rights. I knew what he was doing as a puppet master and a fight promoter, and I could make a case against him. Instead, I waited in silence until he finally looked at me.

"What's going on with this bullshit?" I asked him.

"I don't know what you're talking about."

"The whole school climate is all fucked up," I told him. "Nick's being put in a bad position." I got up and looked down at him. He looked more grown up than he had that day I arrested his father. "Murph," I said softly, "either talk to me now or talk to me later at the police station. It's all the same to me."

"Is that a threat?"

"It's reality. Talk to me now with Nick here, or talk to me later. I'm not wasting my time. Better things to do."

Murphy pointed to Nick. "I'll see you after my next class."

"That will work," Nick said.

To me, Murph said, "Now you're dismissed." The kid walked out like he hadn't a care in the world.

"Sweet kid," I told Nick.

Nick could be the most reasonable person on the planet, and the last thing he expected anyone to do was cross him. He was in a silent state of rage as I left.

After leaving his office, I discovered that Facebook was going crazy. Rumors were taking on a life of their own. We were waiting for the big fight. We knew it was coming, and I just hoped it wasn't at school. I knew Murph was involved in it.

Murph's friend, who Denny had called a fag, was threatened by Mac, one of Denny's friends. Mac became Denny's guardian angel. Unbeknownst to anyone, he was following Denny, thinking that he was going to get jumped. Mac was a big kid, over six feet. A nice kid.

The rumors continued to grow. Everybody was telling me—staff members, random kids, snitches—that today was the day.

The day never came.

I watched Denny very closely. And I watched the kid Denny called a fag. I wasn't sure if those two were going to fight, or if Mac and the fag's brother were going to fight, or if each was going to have their own little militia. I just knew that tension in the school was building. The climate of the school was scary. Everyone was on edge. Kids were misbehaving.

I called Murph into my office.

"I don't want to talk," he said.

"We'll do it here, or we'll do it at the police station," I said, repeating what I had told him earlier. "Let's take a walk."

His friend, Tom, came along, and we took a walk. That's how I wanted it. Two versions of this meeting, not just Murph's. In my experience, if there were two people, the conversation was going to spread on the grapevine in two directions. At that time, MySpace was still pretty popular with the kids, with Facebook taking over, and I wanted it to get out in two different ways. I didn't want just Murph's version.

"Where do you see yourself in five years?" I asked him.

"I don't know."

"Are you going to graduate from high school?"

He shrugged. "I don't care."

With Murph, it was a case of emotional judo. I was trying to get information, so I handed him a piece of paper.

"What the fuck is this?" he shouted.

"You can read."

"Are you arresting me?"

"Murph, that's a complaint application," I said. "Contributing to the delinquency of a minor, trespassing, and assault and battery with a deadly weapon. Also shod foot, which means a kick, becomes a deadly weapon when it's booted." I even threw in kidnapping because of Denny—the way that they'd moved him into the pit when they beat him.

"This is all bullshit," he said, but I could tell I'd gotten to him. "It's not going to work because I finished my probation for stealing that bicycle. Besides, nobody's going to testify against me."

"Murph," I said, trying to sound casual. "You know what makes police powerful?"

"Sure. You have guns."

I checked mine. Yeah, I still had it. "Not just that, Murph. We control information. We gather information. You may think I'm the only police officer in the school. But I have information from hundreds of police officers and databases. I called your probation officer myself. He revoked your probation. A probable cause report."

Murph was a narcissist, stroking his own ego by controlling these kids. But now I had him. I let him read the complaint application. Tom wasn't saying much.

"End this bullshit and, if nothing catastrophic happens, I'll hold onto this piece of paper, and it won't go anywhere," I told him. "If something does happen, you're fried. I'll personally arrest you."

We continued to walk. At this point, I was *Officer Hobson*. Murph wasn't as rude and I sensed a little bit of pleading respect on his part. We finished our walk.

Finally, we had a few days of very tentative peace in the school. Everyone was wary, but it was pretty quiet. In a school that big, quiet is unnerving.

We had assemblies for these kids by grade. The principal would talk. Then I would discuss the consequences of certain crimes and offer a pep talk on good behavior, hoping they would sense the gravity of the situation. I spent some time in the Zoo. They were the kings and queens of social media. They fed the rumors.

After that, I was always watching Murphy like a shadow, but I let him know that I was on his trail.

One day, in the hall, he thought I was spying on him. It was happenstance, we'd just hit it at the same time, but he was too paranoid to believe that.

"You'd better either advise me of my fucking rights and arrest me," he yelled, "or leave me alone. I can't live like this."

"You have the right to remain silent," I said. "And I suggest you shut the fuck up."

Nick called me at home that night. "Murph is back in the Castle," he said. "He's withdrawn from school."

Although he'd left the school, there were other parents whose kids had been hurt in the fight club who wanted justice. And they wanted justice from Murphy.

After a while, I was able to calm them down, explaining to them that he was in a rehab facility and never returning to school. The threat was gone, but the damage was done.

In retrospect, I should have arrested him the first time, but I believed in giving kids a chance. I remembered the kid I had tried to calm after showing up on the domestic violence call all of those years ago.

Murphy was an alcoholic as were his parents. Perhaps he found help in the Castle, but the last I heard anything about him, it looked like he wouldn't be back. And it always hurt to lose one.

✆✄✆

After-thoughts: Shrinking Murphy's Head:

Being a teenager is difficult. But being a teenager with substance abuse issues and living in a house infected with long-standing domestic violence can have devastating, life-long effects. Teens living with domestic violence face the unique problem of trying to fit in with their peers while keeping their home life a secret. Needless to say, their family relationships can be strained to the breaking point. The result can be that these unfortunate kids never learn to form trusting, lasting relationships and many end up in violent relationships themselves, as an assailant, a victim, and everything in between—changing roles and absorbing pain in a no-win life-style.

Like Murphy, these unfortunate sons formulate their own theories about relationships and peer-bonding. Murphy witnessed the cycle of family violence firsthand, initially as a silent and hidden victim cowering from the noise and frightened by the fighting of his parents. He grew into a victim of hands-on abuse when he was old enough to take his mother's side, a victim by association at the hands of his father. Through those damaging and formative years, he learned many physical and emotional defensive mechanisms, designed to offer him an edge in handling the effects of repeated abuse—all this evolving into his puppet-master mentality, his puppets being his impressionable, lower-class mates. He relished his position as a fight promoter, feeding off the power, blood, and raw anxiety of his charges, internalizing the elation of winning and the agony of defeat. Seeing others hurt made him stronger and stroked his ego as he tried to get even, within his universe, at the expense of others.

In Murphy's case, he manipulated younger students, baiting them with the association of a cool kid, membership in a cool clique controlled by the self-professed Jesse James of the school, with promised access to a car, alcohol, and girls. But a ticket to this teenage paradise was not cheap. Admission was contingent upon embracing the fight club and crossing over to the dark side.

But Murphy's malfunctions betrayed him. In his quest to control his personal demons by transferring all of his pain and guilt and debilitating self-worth issues, he failed to understand that good kids with loving families were not good candidates for assimilation into his tortured world. He would find no peace, no happiness in causing their injuries or messing with their naïve sense of things. One of his major mistakes was his inability to see and feel the circumstances of the crimes he was committing, thinking he was an untouchable ring leader.

The bigger they are, the harder they fall and, in Murphy's case, the size of his influence was nothing but an arcane and tragic illusion.

CHAPTER 9

The Battle on Staircase 7

It's been said that between classes, in the halls of any large school, the movement of students resembles that of a herd. Escape panic is a dangerous consequence of herd behavior, but students have free will, and that sets them apart from animals. But because each student is unique, his or her individual response to horror, shock, and repulsion is unpredictable.

Escape panic is fueled by emotions and, as such, a student herd might attempt to move faster than normal. Interactions between individuals become physical. Exits become arched and clogged. Escape is slowed by fallen members serving as obstacles. Individuals display a tendency toward mass or copied behavior.

On a crisp Thursday afternoon, about fifteen minutes before the end of the school day, a student herd formed. Very quickly, that herd became terrified and unnerved. It moved in force toward the largest exit in the building, the front door. That's where I was, standing—at the front door.

In an investigation, you have to work backward. In this new high school, we were very safety-minded, very proactive in its design. We needed to be able to communicate in case of emergency. Every door and every staircase had a number, such as Door 16, Staircase 7.

That Thursday, "the hockey player," the brother of the kid Denny had called a homo, had been taunting Denny all day.

"Fight me here, you pussy. I'll fucking kill you, you piece of shit," and other violently colorful taunts peppered his conversation that morning.

These come-ons were witnessed by countless kids all through the school. Throughout the day, Mac, Denny's friend, was late for a lot of his classes because he was making sure Denny got to classes without any major violence breaking out in the hallways. But Mac wasn't just protecting Denny. He was preparing for the worst. In his backpack, he had secreted a crowbar and a hammer with a metal cap on it.

These were weapons in search of a victim.

At a quarter-to-two on Thursday, with only fifteen minutes left in the school day, the final bell had rung, and kids headed for their homerooms. I was at the end of the hall, almost at the front door of the building, watching the school buses pull in and making sure parents weren't blocking the fire entrances as they usually did.

I was a hundred or more yards away from the staircase when I heard it—the movement, like an eruption or an earthquake. The hairs on the back of my neck tingled and came alive, and my ears rang as if something had exploded inside my head. I heard hundreds of terrified voices, screaming and yelling, loudly and nonsensically, unnatural sounds for a school.

In a panic, I looked straight down the hall. The kids were running from Staircase 7 straight toward me. Instinctively and without knowing what was happening, I pulled my police radio and called for backup. I also called an ambulance, doing so on auto-pilot. It was so quick and so bizarre that I knew this was bad, and that I couldn't handle it alone.

"I have a disturbance," I told the dispatcher, "that involves many students, and I need some help."

I knew the nearby patrol cars would hear it as soon as the dispatcher did, and they would get over there immediately. By calling an ambulance, I'd get the fire department there, too.

A tsunami of kids swept toward me, almost trampling each other. They were pushing and shoving each other. As I ran down the main hall, I had to break up these little scrimmages as I moved along. Like a salmon trying to swim upstream, I fought my way through the crowd to see what was going on.

"Get out of the way," I yelled.

Nobody paid any attention. Everybody was screaming as they swept down the hall toward the front door. It was as close to mob panic as I had ever seen.

Finally, I stepped onto the staircase and my heart dropped. Immediately in front of me lay the hockey player, on his back with blood pooling around his head. Thick red artery blood, I suspected. I wasn't sure of his name at the moment, but I recognized him. Walter, Wally to everyone else. He was splayed out, his body contorted at an unnatural angle. A teacher was there along with another student who had taken off his varsity football sweatshirt and put it under the hockey player's head, trying to stop the bleeding.

Walter was semiconscious.

I scooped the inside of his mouth to keep his airway open and tried not to move him. As I knelt beside him, I heard the sirens coming.

Then next to his body, I saw a hammer.

"Who?" I demanded.

"Mac," one of the kids said. "He went that way." He pointed toward the front entrance, the direction the student herd had gone. "Jack, he had both hands on the hammer, you know, like how you try to ring the bell at the fair, crashing it down with all your strength. That's how he hit Wally, two-fisted on top of his head."

I put the hammer into my belt. It had a long handle, easy to grab two-handed, consistent with what I was just told.

Shit, Mac must have passed me in the hall.

What had happened on the staircase had been happening when I first saw that mob coming toward me.

The staircase was about twelve-feet wide, with a railing in the middle. It was ten steps up to the landing then another ten steps up to the second floor.

I couldn't allow any more students to come down the stairs, not with such a nasty crime scene in progress. I didn't want them to have to pass the blood and the body. The ones who had seen it had run past me, the carnage fueling their panic and flight instinct.

Those first on the scene to help had completely blocked the door at the bottom of the stairs. Like in the movie, *The Poseidon Adventure*, their only egress was up. But to accomplish that I had to clear the staircase, get a few students out at the door next to the victim, and then block that doorway to all except emergency personnel.

The ambulance was calling me for an exact location. At this point, I was trying to remain relatively calm, hoping that my training would kick in. My main objective was getting this herd upstairs and down another staircase, since the bottom stairwell was cluttered by people attending to the victim. But I still had a few stragglers that needed to be evacuated. A few were pushed down and out into the main hallway. At the same time I was directing about thirteen kids up, back the way they came.

I answered the ambulance, "Door 16, behind the loading dock," I yelled into the mic. "The victim is at the bottom of Staircase number 7."

Door 16, the vestibule inside, and the staircase were what I called a vortex of terror. It was on par with Bus 13. Kids were caught fighting, making out, and doing any number of other inappropriate acts there. I was constantly monitoring that place. If I believed in bad karma, I'd say the place was loaded with it.

Now the worst of many nasty incidents had occurred in that location.

Simultaneously, I began yelling commands. I enlisted a couple of big kids, football players, to block the entrance at the bottom of the stairs. I pointed to three students, who were cautiously descending, and yelled, "After these three, nobody gets out this way and nobody gets in, except for adults, staff, and police," I told them. "Nobody. Hold the line, guys."

The students complied, taking their best protect-the-quarterback stances. I headed upstairs a few feet at a time, like a soldier on a battle field trying to claim and secure ground. Up I went, but the stairs were narrowed by the congestion, a bottleneck of frightened humanity. A girl was sitting down, bleeding from her nose and mouth. Friends tended to her. I looked up on the second landing and spotted a bunch of boys in full battle mode, punching each other in total textbook mob panic. Kids kicked and stomped others who had fallen to the ground. Other kids had pulled the shirts of their opponents over their heads and were pummeling them without mercy, like a classic hockey fight. Girls screamed and punched each other wildly, swinging at no one in particular, just frantic perpetual defensive motions. I was pushed to the ground, I can't tell you how many times.

I estimated about thirty students in this very small claustrophobic space. Like a mixed-martial-arts cage match, but much more intense and very real. I had no clue how I was going to stop it.

Then my training and experience kicked in. Suddenly, I was yelling, "Get the fuck out. Go up. Go up and out. Up, out, and down the other staircase. Get off this staircase. Get into the hallway."

The sea of enraged kids paid me no heed. Their voices were strained, loud, and disconnected. Shouts and squeals buzzed from near and far, spreading fear like wildfire. A lot of them knew what had happened and many had heard that a boy had died. They were alarmed, frightened, and, as I would later discover, fighting for their lives. I had to stop them with language they understood.

The fire alarm.

I went for it and pulled. The elevator alarm began to ring. All heads turned, processing the sound.

Maria, the school nurse, appeared like magic on the staircase, tending to the injured girl. She stood and joined the redirection of the crowd. "Up. Go up," she shouted, pushing and pointing.

In the stairwell, the alarm echoed, the shrill sound snapping the kids out of their panic.

"Evacuate the staircase now," I screamed.

The nurse and others were tending to causalities on the staircase, bloody noses, scrapes, cuts, bruises, emerging black eyes, bloody lips, as well as emotional trauma. Stress. Anxiety. Battle fatigue. Paramedics were putting pressure boots on the victim, inserting an IV line for fluids. I was praying it wasn't as bad as it looked, because it looked like death.

I grabbed a fireman, a friend, before he could follow protocol and sound a second alarm. "I pulled the alarm. Don't call a second one," I told him. "There's no fire."

He wasn't happy about the alarm, but when he saw how serious the situation was, he and the other firemen began helping the police calm the kids down and get them out.

Kids began texting and calling their parents, and of course, parents assumed the worst. They descended on the school. We didn't tell them what was happening, just said it was under control.

It wasn't.

I knew every inch of the school, every doorway, like the back of my hand. The police officers did not. But we had to sweep the school before we locked it down. When I told them where to go, they just looked at me confused. In the administrative office, I gave them maps of the school with the staircases marked on them.

Thirteen minutes. From the start of the stampede to the evacuation of the last combatant on the staircase, only thirteen minutes had passed. But I felt like I had aged ten years at least.

The stairs were finally cleared, quiet and still, but littered like the aftermath of a rowdy rock concert.

"Which way did Mac go?" I asked one of the kids.

None of them spoke up.

Teachers in the hall pointed toward the Guidance Office, that big, all-glass suite of rooms. Mac was inside, his guidance counselor in there with him.

I entered the office, followed by two very impatient police officers. My guys, good guys. I still had the hammer wedged into my gun belt, ominous and bloody. Kristen, the principal, was there, pacing, arms folded, impatient, and confused—not approaching Mac but not backing away. She looked at me and her eyes said it all.

She was in charge, but she didn't know what had happened. Looking directly at Mac, but speaking to Kristen, I said, "We're going to take Mac into custody."

He was crying and pacing like a cornered animal. He wasn't even in control yet. "I didn't mean to do it, Jack."

I approached him. "Mac, drop your backpack."

"Officer Hobson, I didn't mean to do it."

"Mac, drop your backpack," I repeated in an even tone.

He was tensing, about to panic, overcome by fear, terror, rage, and regret. I've seen it before. Adrenaline peaks, crashes, then replenishes itself. He was going to run, not away, but around—releasing energy like a pig in a pen, around and around. We couldn't let him move. We had to contain his trajectory or we'd have to fight to contain him.

I was yelling now, not caring that we had an audience looking through the glass from the hallway. "Mac, on the ground, now. Do it. Now." I walked toward him, arms out to the side, closing an escape angle. He was looking through me—no, beyond me. I glanced where his eyes were focused and saw my two back-up officers, their hands on the butts of their 40mm automatic weapons, holsters unsnapped, ready to draw. They were calm, serious, professional, and not fucking around.

This was about to end.

Mac looked back and forth very quickly, like the heads in the audience watching a tennis match. He was frightened, overwhelmed, and out-numbered. I walked slowly toward him. Kristen backed away. My back-up officers matched my forward advance. Mac was being boxed in, a police tactic to prevent escape. He went to his knees, covered his face, and screamed.

It was over. Mac collapsed on the floor. We pounced on him and quickly cuffed him, then rushed him out a side door, and took him to the police station.

Back at the station, we found Denny's class schedule in Mac's backpack. The hammer was processed and placed into evidence. Mac hadn't known how he was going to get to the hockey player. He just found an opportunity to do what he did when he happened to find himself on the staircase with the guy. A crime of opportunity, a happenstance.

Our victim, Wally, was in stable condition. The kid was hit once, hard, in the middle of the top of the head. A lateral wound, six-inches, from the top on his head down, blood oozing from the impact point, his cowlick. It took twenty-two staples to close the wound. He had a concussion, hairline fracture of his cheekbone—most likely caused as he hit the floor face-first—and a sprained neck from his dead-weight forward collapse.

Wally was hit from behind, sucker-thumped. He had no recollection of who hit him.

Mac, a good kid, defending the honor of his friend, Denny, had just hit the big time. I knew Mac. I liked Mac. But I had to charge him with attempted murder, deadly weapon violations, inciting a riot, disrupting a school, and a litany of other offenses. He was transported to the courthouse. High bail was set, twenty-five thousand dollars, and he was held as his parents were unable to facilitate his release. Mac never returned to school. He spent four months in lock-up.

In Massachusetts, one is considered a juvenile until reaching their seventeenth birthday. Juveniles are afforded certain protections under the law, and juvenile procedures differ greatly from the adult process. Ironically, Mac had turned seventeen three days before the Battle on Staircase 7.

The aftermath of these incidents sent shock waves throughout the community. Media coverage was intense. Students were counseled and debriefed. Teachers, those first on-the-scene, had issues, nightmares they'd tell me. I told them that they performed magnificently under pressure. My friend Maria, the nurse, appeared as unaffected as I was, but it was just a facade. We met for cocktails with other teachers to talk through our anxiety.

Some parents removed their children from school, seeking a less dangerous environment.

I visited Mac in lock-up a couple of times because I liked him and because he was alone and frightened. I was never his enemy, but he knew that my police report and testimony would sink him. His life was in turmoil. He was generally hated and vilified by his peers. Sticks and stones might break your bones, but names will hurt you more. The incident all boiled down to name calling.

A bad decision takes two seconds. The pain it causes might last a lifetime.

In the Battle on Staircase 7, there were no winners.

CHAPTER 10

Ryan: The Hulk

I knew the Battle on Staircase 7 had a potential for great violence. So did the unrequited love story of the Hulk. While no Romeo and Juliet, it was a love story, at least from The Hulk's point of view.

They met in the summer, and he was Janie's first boyfriend. He would slip out at night and go to her house. The two of them were picked up by police on one of those nights as they walked around town. It was an innocent attraction for her but an obsession for him.

His name was Ryan, but I called this kid The Hulk for good reason. Although he wasn't very tall, he was solid as a rock with a neck like a wrestler, his back and shoulders strong for a kid his age.

When I first shook Ryan's hand, I noticed that his fists were bigger than mine, fists like the Incredible Hulk, though not green, of course. My dad had taught me at an early age the importance of a firm handshake and shined shoes. "When you shake hands, make your grip firm, and look the other person square in the eye," he'd tell me. "Don't look down or away. To some, that's a sign of weakness. First impressions," he'd say, "they can make or break you."

I made it a point to shake hands with all the kids, to show them how a handshake was supposed to feel. I extended mine to the Hulk. "Ryan, do you know why people shake hands?" No response. "It's to show the other person that your hand is empty and that you're not a threat, that you're not carrying a weapon."

His shake was firm, his grip tight. The Hulk didn't need any instruction in that department. However, the only attempt at eye contact was mine. Still gripping his hand, I turned it over and saw a calcified middle knuckle, much bigger than the other, and permanent.

"Do you box, Ryan?" I asked.

"No," he said.

"Been in a lot of street fights, maybe?"

"A few," he said.

I released his hand and we parted ways. I shook my head. What I had seen was called a boxer's knuckle. It happens when punches are thrown and connect without gloves or wraps—bare fists, like a street fighter's—and it only happens after numerous fights. I was a boxer, and now I was more than curious, as well as a bit disturbed when I thought about it.

One morning, Janie and the Hulk had been spotted together in the otherwise vacant cafeteria. The day before, I'd sat in on a meeting with Janie, her parents, and Diana, her guidance counselor. The meeting was called because Janie was frightened about Ryan's controlling and, sometimes, very mean behavior. His anger, she told us, was spontaneous and unpredictable. Ryan was pressuring her to run away and, by bus or by train, find their way to South Carolina, where he had relatives, some eight-hundred miles away.

We discussed, at great length, the reasons behind an abuse protections order—a 209A—and the legal consequences for its violation by the defendant, Ryan.

I presented them with all the necessary documents, everything in order, wrapped in a neat little packet. "Take this to courthouse, present it the clerk and, on Janie's behalf, a court order will be issued. Then I'll have the leverage of arrest powers, and we can end this."

Letting Janie sit in on our discussion proved to be a mistake. Each time I spoke about Ryan's consequences if the order was violated, her eyes would water up, and she would plead with me to reconsider keeping them apart. Trying to appeal to the common sensibilities of a love-stricken, fourteen-year-old girl was like throwing a rock down an empty well and waiting for the splash.

That was the day before and, as of the next morning, I had no verbal or concrete documentation that a 209A had been issued, so erring on the side of caution, I sent her one way and him the other.

Afterward, while I was in the front office, one of the teachers' emergency lights flashed on the switchboard.

"Jack," the counselor said. "We have a light on the second floor, room 202, last room on the left, biology wing."

I realized that was where Janie had headed. As I left, the lights from classrooms adjacent to room 202 started blinking.

Not an accident. Trouble!

I glanced at my watch. Seven forty-five a.m. "Awesome!"

As I hit the stairs, taking two at a time with a surge of adrenaline, I couldn't shake the feeling of impending doom. An assistant principal caught up to me, and his eyes said it all as we entered the hallway.

The classroom was at the very end of the hall. As we ran toward it, we spotted glass on the floor. At first glance, it looked like someone had knocked over an aquarium, shattering it into a million pieces. But there was no water or fish to confirm the theory.

On the floor, about three feet inside of room 202, the history teacher was struggling to his feet, like a prize fighter trying to beat the count before the bell. His scalp was bleeding. He was out of breath, hyperventilating, and pissed off. Splintered wood, large chunks of glass, and blood littered the threshold. Other teachers gathered around, trying to get him comfortable, applying towels to his head.

The teacher was disoriented. Not the kids, though. The violence perpetuated through video games, raunchy music lyrics, horror and slasher movies, combined with nonstop real-life depictions of death and war around the world, had invaded and bombarded their perception of brutality. Their generation, their violently apathetic culture, that I called *the age of rage*, had desensitized too many of them. Kids had become accustomed to bloody bodies dropping to the floor then being reanimated as immortal zombies that fought on and on.

But not today. This was not a game. They remained in their seats, stunned but not visibly upset. EMS, fire, and police were now at the scene. Another teacher had assumed control of the class. I waved Janie out of the room, grabbed her backpack, then walked her to an empty class room to talk.

"Janie," I said. "Do we have a restraining order?"

"I don't know," she replied without making eye contact.

"You'll be fine," I told her. "I'm going to have you dismissed for the day, but first tell me what happened after you left the cafeteria."

"He followed me and grabbed my backpack from behind, pulled me down to the floor. I hit the back of my head." She then told me that a couple of big kids, probably seniors, helped her up. "One of them pushed Ryan down. I snuck through the crowd and ran to class."

"How long before Ryan showed up?"

"I don't know. Ten minutes maybe?"

As Janie turned to leave with Diana, her counselor, I said, "Have her head checked out because she could be hurt. And arrange for her mom or dad to pick her up."

"No problem," she told me. "We're all afraid of this kid, Jack."

"I know. I'll have him cuffed and out of the school within an hour or less, no worries."

I tried to talk to the teacher as he was triaged and put on a stretcher.

"It was that boy, Ryan," he said. "He came knocking on the door and wanted to see this girl. I told him he wasn't supposed to be here and to get out." He calmed down then explained how he had picked up his phone to call for assistance, leaning away from the door as the Hulk began hammering on it. "He banged and kicked so hard that the hinges gave, and the glass broke in one big heavy pane and crashed onto my head."

My mind went in a million directions. This kid had a problem, a major malfunction. I knew his father, and I knew his father had guns, collected them actually. It added up to the worst case scenario, which I had been trained to handle but did my best to prevent. Easier said than done.

The teacher was being strapped into the stretcher and I placed a hand on his shoulder. "I will check in on you later. I have to take care of this now."

As the stretcher was taken to the elevator, a teacher ran up to me. "Jack, I don't know what's going on," he said. "Ryan's in one of the empty rooms on the far end of the science wing. He's smashing tables, breaking things, and yelling."

On instinct, I called the front office to announce a school-wide soft lockdown—a stay-in-place, in which teachers and students go about their business in the classroom, but no one leaves. Anyone in the halls is directed to the nearest supervised classroom. Attendance is taken—the whereabouts of wandering students to be dealt with after the all-clear announcement. We weren't there quite yet. In this soft lock-down, staff is trained to disregard bells or alarms. When the coast is clear or when the threat is extinguished, we will "release" the school, and classes resume.

I called the station on my cell phone and requested a back-up. In an attempt to ease my tension, I turned to Nick, the assistant principal who looked as tense as I felt. "He's really fucking up our coffee time, isn't he?"

We headed for the stairs. With every step, I prepared myself for the confrontation, hoping that my police training would kick in, instinctual and focused. One thing was certain. I would do whatever was necessary to keep this kid from hurting anyone else.

We reached the top of the stairs, and, as we approached the hallway, we could hear the sounds of metal on metal and glass breaking. *A bull in a china shop*, I thought while running to the door of the classroom. Inside was the Hulk, red faced and pacing with fists clinched. As I assessed the situation, I thought about Ryan, my past experiences with him, and his thought process. He was always respectful of my uniform, but he was only fifteen-years-old and not fully emotionally developed.

There were a few behavioral theories that seemed to have converged into a perfect storm within Ryan, creating a volatile mix of emotion, arousal, and violence. When I think critically about his behavior, I think first of *choice theory,* which simply contends that behavior is a rational choice made by a motivated offender who perceives that the chances of gain outweigh any possible punishment or loss. Ryan was told, face-to-face, of the severe consequences of his obsessive behavior, arrest being my preferred response, but that didn't seem to sink in.

Next, two macro-theories, small but important factions of emerging violent behavior, one called *trait* and the other *arousal,* suggest that a delinquent's actions are impulsive or instinctual rather than rational. Arousal theory suggests that rash decisions, controlled by real-time environmental stimuli, create a sensation stimulating violent activities.

As the components of these behaviors united into an obsessive rage, Ryan's emotional trigger was pulled, fueled by excitement and adrenaline. It replaced rational thought with extreme and violent behavior. But these were only my ideas about theories within theories and symptoms of individual, internal conflict. No one can really predict behavior or reactions to it—theories are just a calculated best guess. Ryan's actions spoke louder than words. He had assaulted a teacher, destroyed property, disrupted an entire school, and pissed me off. The Hulk was a textbook come to life. But I am a police officer, and I'd had enough.

The door to the room was closed but unlocked. With the assistant principal behind me, I opened the door dramatically and displayed my version of shock and awe. Using my cop voice, I told Ryan to get his ass down. I continued to bombard him with my commands. Moving closer to him as I spoke, I pushed aside desks and chairs for theatrical effect, toning down his rage to confusion and fear.

We all learn that, when faced with dangerous and life-threatening situations, our fight or flight instincts kick in. Fight or flee. But there's one more possible outcome. We freeze, crippled and paralyzed by fear. This was how Ryan reacted. His mouth opened, and his body tensed as if frozen or stuck in concrete. Still shouting, I positioned my handcuffs, and, with a motion like throwing a Frisbee, I moved behind him, and pushed him to the ground. There, I placed a knee on his back and grabbed his wrists.

Then I became a bull rider, with the Hulk being the bull. He stood up and shook me off.

The assistant principal, on instinct, joined the battle followed by another teacher and a hall monitor. We all grabbed a piece of that remarkably strong and panic-fueled fifteen-year-old.

Then, suddenly, he was done. Outnumbered, exhausted, and defeated, he dropped. The rage was fading from his eyes, his body relaxing. Once he was handcuffed, we all exhaled. Then the police cavalry showed up—better late than never. Ryan was dragged out of the classroom, down the stairs, under arrest. He never returned to school.

This was one of those situations I couldn't help, a time when the law had to take over. It wasn't the way I liked to see a story end, but it was the only way the Hulk's could. This wasn't a case of my calming a kid down, taking him for a walk, trying to talk sense into parents, or even rearranging the facts so someone could have a second chance. The Hulk had run out of second chances, and now he was going to have to deal with the real and rigid world of the juvenile justice system.

CHAPTER 11

The Alliance

Not every situation I came across had to do with fights, threats, blood, and gore at the school. Some of the kids were grappling with private issues, and among them was sexual orientation.

Students in the Gay, Lesbian, Bi-sexual, and Transgender Alliance (GLBT) met every Thursday afternoon in the art room, an open gallery space where kids worked on everything from ceramics and metal sculpture to drawing and painting.

I'd volunteered to help out as an advisor to the organization and liked to visit the space often. I was amazed to see what kids could do once they enrolled in an art class. I watched some of our meekest students blossom in this environment.

The kids would send photos to me on their phones of their activities outside of school, but I had no idea if they actually were where they said they were. I would always reply, "Be careful" or "Don't get in trouble and say No to drugs!"

Gail, the teacher, had a lot of GLBT kids in her classes and allowed them to use her room for their meetings. Thin and attractive with long brown hair, Gail was admired all over the area as a working artist. She looked to be in her early fifties, with the earthy smile kids instinctively trusted. Married to a teacher in a nearby district, she was clearly dedicated. Students had been gravitating to her for months, talking to her about their problems in a way they hadn't done before with other members of the faculty.

I liked to tease her about her passion for her job. "You're not covered with paint today, Gail," I'd say. "Anything wrong?"

Typically wearing overalls or jeans, she was usually splattered head-to-toe with paint. "Just give me time, Jack," she'd say. "It's early yet."

And then I'd watch her motivate her class, the energy in the room building as she tended to her students one by one.

The Alliance, as it was referred to at school, met every Thursday afternoon, and I tried my best to be there. The more I got to know these kids, the better I understood them. Yes, they were all individuals, but many had overlapping histories. Some were cutters, kids who used a blade on themselves as their way of dealing with anguish. By cutting themselves, they thought they could control their pain because it was a real and tangible thing and when they bled, they purged themselves of everything toxic, at least that's what some of my cutters told me. Many were drug users. Some were drug enthusiasts and were experimenting with altered states. A few had overdosed and been revived, narrowly escaping death. At least half of them had been committed to sleep-over facilities—court- or doctor-ordered shelters at one time or another. Some had been committed for days or weeks.

Gail gave encouragement to the kids, helping them deal with being bullied or cast aside because of their sexual orientation. She listened to their stories and pushed them to form a support group.

Jenny was a typical Goth girl. Dyeing her hair black and painting her lips and eyelids to match, she'd made her face look hollow, as if she hovered between living and dying. She identified with Marilyn Manson. Everybody gave her a wide path when she walked down the hall. She treated me well enough, but it was obvious she felt being a buddy to a police officer wasn't in her best interests. Other Goth kids made an effort to sit near her at lunch. Huddling like outcasts in their antiquated dress and sharing their dark-shaded music, they seemed to be hiding in plain sight from the rest of the student body. For weekend kicks, they attended Goth Fests in Boston, a twenty-minute drive away.

A known cutter, Jenny was one of the few kids to whom I'd given my phone number. I wanted her to know she could confide in me. She'd confessed that she was the black sheep in her family, that with her two brothers off to college and competing in sports, she felt tossed aside, the loser of the bunch. Most kids outgrew the Goth stage as soon as they were involved with their first serious crush, thinking twice about appearing in their undertaker gear and bizarre makeup when meeting their date's family. I wanted Jenny to be one of those kids. I was afraid she might get so deep into the Goth lifestyle she wouldn't be able to get out. I was afraid she'd meet up with other outcasts who were drifting toward crime, and they would drag her into their bad decisions. Guilt by association.

She never used my number to talk to me, but she did send me photos of her with her friends. "See, Jack?" she texted on those occasions, "I'm still alive."

⊰⊱

Brian was a cross-dresser. He used make up and wore silk scarves. At five-feet-two and barely one-hundred pounds soaking wet, he'd wear a blue sneaker on one foot, red on the other. He furthered this statement by painting his eyelids to match. Effeminate in manner, he enjoyed the attention he got. I would tell him all the time that he was giving the Knuckleheads in the school ammunition to taunt and bully him.

He would say, "Ya, but I look good."

"Beauty's in the eye of the beholder," I would say, shaking my head in dismay.

He was very much a sheep, taking himself to the slaughter. After being continually harassed in school and out, and a prime target for faraway laughter, he'd learned to attack. His cruelty could be devastating, causing many bullies to stop in their tracks. He'd been to therapy more than once.

I was called upon to remove him from class one day for acting out. "You didn't take your Ritalin today, did you?" I asked.

"No," he answered honestly.

I took him to our school nurse, Maria.

Never one to dress in uniform, she ruled this state-of-the-art office with a warm approach. I'd known and admired her for three decades. There were numerous times we dealt with students suffering from serious mental health issues. Staying an arm's length away from the administration, we were a tough tag team.

As usual, she greeted us with a calm, assuring smile. We'd been through this before with Brian, calling him our Ritalin Ranger. He, like many students I called the Fakers, used this office as a sanctuary away from tests and assignments.

I turned to him and gave him a look I hoped would loosen him up. "You wouldn't be the first to play sick on a test day," I told him. "Hell, I used to try that once in a while when I was a kid."

To Brian's credit, he wasn't faking.

Maria took charge. Leading him toward a bed where he could lie down, she administered medicine prescribed especially for him.

ↄ⌀ↄ

One of Maria's favorite patients was Brian's boyfriend, David. He suffered from panic attacks that carried all the symptoms of a heart seizure. Whenever they occurred, we took him by stretcher to the nurse's office. If he didn't start showing signs of recovery, we'd call an ambulance and have him rushed to the hospital. Unlike Brian, David wasn't a member of the Alliance. A senior, he had a six-foot frame that was well muscled under a layer of fat. He was known for the attention he paid to his curly black hair, his impeccable clothing, and the nice car he drove.

One day, Maria called me from her office. "Can you come quickly, Jack?" she said. "I've got David here and I'm going to need you."

When I got there, David was in a wheelchair, gray-faced and trying to breathe into a paper bag. Maria had already given him his prescribed medication. The Fakers were all in their beds. Nick, the vice principal, was there. I rolled David away from the center of attention. I'd learned that if I could get him talking, he tended to come around and settle down.

His story came in spurts. "My boyfriend," he said.

"Your boyfriend, Brian?"

"Yes." Tears coursed down his cheeks. "Last night he punched me."

I looked for marks on his face. None. In Massachusetts a punch from a partner is domestic violence, even if it involves a pair of teens. When I started to inform him about his rights as a victim, he started crying harder. He was scared now, and I didn't know if I'd helped or increased his anxiety. For David, reality took a quick and ugly turn into the world of consequences, the outcomes of which could annihilate his fragile relationship with Brian.

Maria eyed me. "You better know what you're doing, Jack."

"Yes, of course," I said with a wink. But truth be told, my decisions in this arena were all pretty much a leap of faith.

David stopped sobbing. "I need a cigarette."

The vice principal stepped forward. "You can't smoke on school grounds," he said.

But he can smoke outside in his car, I thought. This was a good time for a change of scenery.

"Good idea." I turned to Maria. "Let me take him for a drive. He needs to calm down."

"Okay," she said. "Just a short one."

There are no secrets in high school. Soon there'd be a dozen messages swapped about this situation. I didn't want David and Brian's spat going viral, so I did my best to keep our actions covert. I casually walked him out to my Cruiser and offered him a seat up front with me. I asked him where he'd parked his car, drove him there, and he retrieved his cigarettes.

While he smoked, I spoke to him about Brian. "You want me to talk to him before you do anything you might regret?"

"He likes you," he said. "But maybe I can handle this myself."

I began driving out of the lot. "I still have to write this up," I told him. "If you were to come to the group, do you think you could talk it out together? It's like Vegas. What happens in that room, stays in that room."

He had to think about that.

I drove him back to school, walked him into the nurse's office, and reported to Maria. "David and I have been talking," I said, "about he and Brian going to group together."

"Sounds good," she said. "How about you, David? Will you agree to that?"

We waited.

"Yes," he finally said.

He seemed to be breathing better and he'd stopped crying. Soon he felt well enough to go back to his classes. After David returned to class, I had a brief conversation with Brian about how relationships are hard and complicated—telling him that sometimes anger causes spontaneous trigger actions and reactions that hurt others. Things like harsh words, verbal attacks to a partner's weak spot, and other mindless stuff that happens when arguments are raw and heated. I said these things to Brian because I knew him and I'd helped him in the past when he was bullied. And he did show up for Thursday's Alliance meeting, eventually laughing and holding hands with David.

I started the meeting with a general conversation about on domestic violence and the aftereffects of violence, clarifying that violence can be physical, emotional, or mental, and under Massachusetts law, violence, however defined, is taken very seriously. "I don't want any of you to feel the heat of a bad decision," I reminded them. "But if any of you commit such an act, the laws are very unforgiving and I'll drag you, crying, to jail." My bad cop routine. This seemed to bring smiles and jeers and looks of immediate personal understanding, as they all seemed to be searching their memory banks, flashing their dating relationships through their minds.

The Alliance kids knew I was on their side, and they also knew I could be a soft touch.

က‍ာ‍တ

William, another kid in the Alliance, looked like a little doughboy. Five-foot-five and overweight, he kept his hair buzzed and proudly walked the halls in the style of a celebrity. On Fridays, he'd dress up in sequins and jewels, wearing tight Spandex body suits that made him look like an overstuffed sausage. Later at night, he'd change again and watch *The Rocky Horror Picture Show* dressed as one of the film's characters.

I have to admit I used him on occasion. An extreme techie, he was a magician with anything cellular or cyber. Hunched over a task to service my computer in his Liberace costume, he looked to be making a fashion statement rather than miming the candelabra queen.

Gail, the art teacher, asked me about boyfriends and girlfriends in the Alliance.

"It can get complicated," I said.

"Just like anywhere else."

"True," I said.

We'd talk about their parents. I'd take off my tie and my bulletproof vest—twenty pounds when combined with my gun belt.

"What's that tattoo on your arm?" she asked.

"A love ode for my wife. Ainei, its means Nancy," I said. "And under the shamrock it reads, "Mo Grai, Mo Saoil, *My love, my life*, in Gaelic."

"Aren't there police rules?" she asked.

"Can't have anything on your neck," I told her, "and you can't have a full sleeve."

The kids were unconsciously flashing their own tattoos.

One day while William was helping me with my computer, he mentioned *The Rocky Horror Picture Show* and I knew there was more to it than that.

"You know what I'm talkin' about?" he asked.

"Why wouldn't I?" I replied. "You run off to watch it every Friday night."

"The movie," he said. "Me and some other kids from Alliance have watched the movie a few hundred times." He moved back from my computer, slapped his hands together like he had mastered his chore. "Now, some of us want to go to The Rocky Horror Show Festival."

That was a surprise. Most of the kids didn't hang together outside of school. They weren't buddies. Generally, the Alliance was a secret meeting after school, period. Group therapy, kindred spirits but not for public view.

"Where?" I asked lamely. "Providence again?"

"Boston."

"Boston?" I chuckled politely. "At a midnight event. How are you going to make that happen?"

He mopped his brow like he'd been working for hours, when in reality he'd been there about ten minutes. "Thought you'd make it happen for us." I knew what he meant. He wanted me to contribute to their travel fund.

I stared at him, utterly dead-pan.

Not discouraged, he waited.

"Listen," I said, after we'd been standing there so long my legs had gone numb. "Maybe I can work out something with the principal. But it would mean all of you would be put to work." I pictured the Alliance in ordinary work clothes, and it took all I had to continue.

"We're talking four stories of rooms that need cleaning, all the windows, the cafeteria, the auditorium, the gymnasium, every square inch of this school."

William did his hand-slapping thing again. "No problem."

"I'll have to talk to every one of your folks."

William nodded in agreement. "Without question."

That was when I felt inwardly defeated a bit. Watching them in my mind, trying to get all their parents involved when most of them hadn't had a meaningful dialogue with them in months was too much for me. I sat down. Maybe the principal would buy it. Hell, why not risk it?

"Whatever you get in the way of money for your labor," I said. "I'll match it."

Almost a month later, I got a text message from Jenny the Goth with a photo of several Alliance members in *Rocky Horror* garb, posing.

It read, "Still alive, Jack."

CHAPTER 12

Angie's Quest for Inclusion

One day, I noticed something out of the ordinary, and it had to do with Angie. Angie was a teenager—a fourteen-year-old, trapped mentally within the sensibilities of an eight-year-old. A psychologist told me that she was functioning with diminished capacity, that affected her decision making, and that her spatial and cognitive abilities were low. I took that to mean that she had a low IQ. That was easier for me to process. She was labeled as special, and she hated it. She took the special bus to school—the short bus, as other kids would taunt. She wanted a friend, a real friend, someone she could talk to, gossip about boys with, and count on when she felt blue and depressed.

Angie was a nice kid who stayed out of trouble. She had tested low and was placed in remedial classes. It was the beginning of the school year, at lunch one day, when I saw her sitting with Britney and some other kids.

What's that about? I wondered.

After lunch was over, Toria, one of the girls from the table, came by my office. It was the way she got out of class, but for me, these visits from students were often a shortcut to a lot of information.

"Some girls are having a sleepover at Britney's house," she told me.

"I'd like to be a fly on the wall for that one."

"At least we'll have some privacy," she said.

It's a school night, strange for a sleep over, I thought.

Britney's house was a big colonial house that the grandmother kept neat and cheerful. Britney's mother, an addict, had her own dark, little corner, and Britney had her run of the rest of it, including her bedroom in the basement.

"You girls behave yourself," I said.

Toria rolled her eyes. "You think I'd be telling you about this if we were going to do anything bad?"

Ya I do, I mused. These were not rocket scientists. "Thanks for letting me know," I said. "You'd better get back to class now."

At the end of the school day, the buses left, and I heard on my police radio that a special-needs girl never made it on the bus. Then I heard her name.

Angie.

At the police station, her parents said she wasn't answering her cell phone. They were panicked. They wanted us to explain where she was and why. We couldn't. Clouds were forming, and wind gusts were becoming strong—a storm that had been forecasted was on its way.

Even if a phone was off, we had no problem finding its last location. But we couldn't ping Angie's, which meant the battery was dead, or someone had taken the phone apart.

As a police officer, I'd been involved in quite a few missing-persons cases, following some searches that had ended with tragedy. I remember that night all too clearly.

We were having a wild tropical storm. The darker it got, the more worried I became. We still couldn't find Angie.

I decided to get on her Facebook page. Kids these days are extremely tech savvy, and apparently, so was she. I couldn't get into her account, so I called her parents and asked if she had friends who could. Soon the boy who lived next door joined us at the station and got into her account. Sure enough, on her Facebook wall, she was bragging about going to a slumber party at a different girl's house, not Britney's. We went to the house, but nothing was going on.

As the night progressed, our late-season storm got worse—rain sideways, flooding the local rivers and streams. I wasn't sure how Angie, or anyone, would handle being out in a storm as violent as this one. This girl had special needs, and her parents were losing their minds with worry.

In situations like this, every community kind of automatically pulls together. We called in canines from other police departments. We put out a missing/endangered warrant on Angie, along with a Q2, which is a stop-and-hold warrant. We organized a big search, involving a lot of people who cared, including off-duty officers and even the police chief.

I continued to search Facebook and discussion walls, looking for any and all information about this sleepover and hoping Angie would find a way to post something herself. I focused on the kids from the Zoo class, who had been seen with Angie. I called the guidance counselor at home to figure out the best way to get in touch with these kids.

The search went on.

Then a break, on Facebook. A lot of kids were talking about the sleepover at Britney's. One kid mentioned Angie's name. I went to his house and spoke to him. He couldn't give me any new information.

"All I know," he said, "is that Angie was happy she was invited to Britney's. She didn't get invited to stuff. I think she was going there, no matter what."

I had already driven by Britney's, but it was clear no one was home. I knew the kind of activity that signaled a sleepover. Parked cars. Parents dropping off kids. Noise, lots of noise. Nothing like that was going on. No one was answering the land line there, either.

The other officers and I started thinking of other possibilities. An abduction. An injury. Or worse.

At about eleven-thirty that night, a picture of Angie and another girl showed up on a Facebook wall, a picture that Britney commented on. That did it. My normally even temper flared. I was beyond pissed off, as were my fellow officers. Without a warrant, we headed to Britney's. I pounded on the door.

Her grandmother opened it a crack. "You can't come in here," she said, more stunned than anything else.

I put my leg in the door and pushed my way in, followed by other police officers, all of us dripping rain from the storm. We were very professional, but in an urgent way. I didn't want to listen to any of the drama. We had tunnel vision on what might have happened, and we had to get to the truth before Angie's situation, assuming she was still alive, got even worse.

The grandmother knew me from before, but she was frightened. I made eye contact and hoped she would remember that I had been there for her family in the past.

"Where's Britney, ma'am?"

She sighed and wrapped her robe tighter. "Down in the cellar with some girls. They're having a sleepover."

We went downstairs. The girls began to scream and cry.

"Get up and put on your clothes," I told them. To Britney, I said, "Where's Angie?"

"I don't know what you're talking about, Officer Hobson."

"Are you having a slumber party?"

"No, just some girlfriends over."

"I know you had a conversation with her. And I know that you gave her your phone number."

"I didn't."

"Okay, then," I said. "Guess we're going to have to get names and numbers from everyone. Are you sure you girls don't know anything about this?"

"Tell him," one of Britney's buddies said. "We did invite Angie, Officer Hobson. We invited a lot of kids. But she didn't come over, and she didn't call. And then a while ago we posted a picture of Angie: a picture from the cafeteria, for a laugh," she admitted.

After the other officers and I left the girls downstairs, I stuck around to talk to the grandmother. The mother even got up and joined us. They were both very worried about Angie and what might have happened to her. I didn't tell them how many times I'd been on the other end of those searches.

Finally, I was convinced Angie had never made it to this sleepover. So where the hell was she?

At daybreak, thirteen hours after starting the search, we still had nothing. Out of the blue, they got a call at the station from a neighbor who lived near Britney's.

"I don't know what to do, but I think there's somebody inside the cab of my tractor," he said.

I was already back at the high school when I got the call on the radio. "We found her. It's the girl."

Angie had become disoriented in her search for the sleepover at Britney's. As the storm had gotten worse, she knocked on doors and spoken to strangers, trying to find Britney's address. Then she had found what she thought was a farmhouse. On her way down a long driveway, the storm made it impossible for her to continue. She spotted the tractor and its large cab and managed to climb up into it. She camped there, without her phone, for six or seven hours. I'm not sure exactly how many hours because not even Angie was sure how long she was there.

I got on the radio directly with the officers who found Angie. I wanted her transported back to the school so the nurse could check her out and send her home or to the hospital if her parents wanted more of an assessment. That was where things got messy.

She was transported back to the police department and examined by the paramedics. Then came the big question. What should we do with her? The warrant we had issued was an endangered child warrant. The police administration had decided to interpret the warrant as a runaway warrant. They wanted to arrest Angie and throw her into the juvenile court, then have her examined psychologically. Sometimes the system is the right way to go. This wasn't one of those times.

I fought their decision in the strongest possible terms. "You just don't do this," I argued. "You don't deal with fourteen-year-old special-needs girls as if she is an adult."

She had a lot of systems and people already put in place for her, acting in her best interest.

But the police administration wouldn't listen. They arrested Angie. She had an anxiety attack and was hospitalized for a few days. Worse, she didn't return to school.

After a couple of weeks of frustration, I called her parents.

"This is ridiculous," I said when we met. "You were doing everything you needed to for your daughter. She had a little misstep, and now she is at the mercy of the court. We need to get her back."

I convinced Angie's parents to sign her back into school. They decided that she'd be transported in a special-needs bus with more accountability, to and from school.

My job didn't end when classes were over for the day. To do the job right, you don't leave at three p.m. when school is out. As many times as I tried to do that, I would inevitably go back in. I didn't have to, but I would because I knew and cared about these kids. While it's not possible to follow their logic or understand their decisions, something I gave up trying to do a long time ago, I could be there for them when they needed me.

At the end of the year, Angie was back in school. She became one of my pals. Her mother called me frequently for updates. We were pals, too.

CHAPTER 13

Britney: Beating the Odds

Britney came with a reputation from middle school. Tiny, petite, another one with long blonde hair, she'd been branded a drama queen, a spoiled brat prone to throwing tantrums. She had no filter and was sent to the Zoo soon after arriving at the school. No one could calm her down. It got to be that I would point her out to others as our permanent resident.

"Where's your books?" I'd ask her.

"I lost them."

"What about your backpack?"

"Too heavy."

"Do you have any money?"

"Nope."

"How are you going to eat?"

"I'll get by."

She was part of a band of students who would grab hamburgers right off the food line without paying. I'd apprehended a few of them and sent them to the principal. Britney was one of the thieves I turned a blind eye to now and then. I did that because I knew she would actually eat the burger, not hoard it like a prize. I knew she was broke and hungry and that her home life was far from ideal. Maybe an extra hamburger now and then would help her make it through to graduation.

On the other hand, the odds were against her. Her frequent trips to the Zoo did little, if anything, to calm her down.

This was a new school with a state-of-the-art cafeteria that featured a buffet like you'd see in a fine restaurant. The salad station, along with fresh greens, offered a selection of fruit and yogurt. The entrée choices might include chicken marsala and stuffed pasta shells. More casual offerings leaned toward fast food—like hamburgers, hot dogs, and fish sandwiches. The deli station was popular as was the desserts set out at the end of the line.

The cafeteria served from ten thirty until noon. Kids on special diets were allowed in first, along with the blind students and special-needs kids. Everyone was given a half-hour to eat. That meant that four floors of students were served daily, one after the other, four to five hundred kids in each section.

The cafeteria was my beat. Because of security concerns, I couldn't be there at any set time, but I was around. Regardless of how appealing the school tried to make it, the crowded environment seemed to breed discontent.

Britney's behavior there could cause problems. Kids were already wound up, and her stealing and constant meltdowns got the attention of Monique, a guidance counselor. Britney became the counselor's pet project.

I kept getting calls from the Zoo about Britney's behavior. When the teacher tried to discipline her, Britney complained to me about being yelled at. When I yelled at her, she wanted to talk to her mother. That was how the chain of command worked.

Monique felt that Britney would benefit from sitting in with the Alliance kids. Even though she wasn't gay, the kids offered kinship and a group-therapy approach that seemed to work for them. One thing was for sure. She needed to change.

One day, I went to get her, and she wasn't there. I heard a commotion down the hall and found her in a room with Monique and the Principal, Kristen McKay. No one could calm her down.

"You're going to have to take her, Jack," Monique said.

I moved fast to where she was sitting defiantly in a chair, screaming and swearing. "Stand up," I said.

She stood, reluctantly.

"Put your hands behind your back."

She complied.

I cuffed her. Without a word to the others, I proceeded to walk her out of the room. When we hit the hall, I purposely slowed my pace so the kids could witness our every step. By the time I got her outside and to my car, she was kicking and screaming. I put her in the backseat and belted her in. *Tough love is a bitch*, I thought.

"You're under arrest for disrupting a school assembly," I said.

"There's no assembly. I didn't do anything."

"That's what it's called. Kids were assembled. You disrupted that assembly. Come on."

Because she was fifteen, I couldn't advise her of her rights without a parent or guardian present.

As I walked her into the booking area of the police station, she was screaming bloody murder. I finally got her calmed down enough that I could do some thinking. I knew she and her mother lived in the basement of her grandmother's house. I also knew that her mother was a drug addict.

"You wanted your mother," I said to her. "Now's a good time to call her."

Twenty minutes later, her mother showed up. Britney was still handcuffed at the booking table, with a female officer and me hovering over her. The mother moved toward us like a zombie.

She had probably shot up on the way to the station. First thing I did was send someone out to see how she got here. That ended up an unnecessary request. The grandmother walked in, grief and anger on her face so telling that my heart sank.

The mother couldn't put two words together. I spotted blood on one of her thighs, probably where she had injected herself.

Britney immediately spun into an anxiety attack. Quickly, I put her and her mom in a vacant room.

"I could arrest you both and make it stick," I told them. "But I've decided to get you both treated."

I called for an ambulance. "I have a forty-two-year-old female and her fifteen-year-old daughter who until this minute were under arrest," I said, making sure Britney was paying attention. "I've decided to transport both of them to the hospital's emergency room."

I'd had it, and I figured we might as well kill two birds with one stone.

Any other police officer probably would have arrested them, but sometimes you have to gamble.

Later, I had to alert the Department of Social Services. There would be forms to fill out. I wanted to put in motion an investigation to see what housing would work best for Britney, with foster care on the back burner. In my view, such a change could be devastating for this fifteen-year-old girl.

True, her mother was a disaster, but she did have a grandmother she was close to.

When she returned to school, she avoided me at every opportunity. She'd gotten a scare, and she knew I was serious.

Britney's story has, if not a happy ending, a satisfying one. Yet after her near arrest, I continued to keep my eye on her. Britney never again crossed my path, but she continued to make guest appearances at the Zoo. All the way through graduation.

ᑯᑫᑯ

An Alternative:

When I was going through my doctoral program, I wrote a grant proposing a new idea for a night school— actually, it was the objective of the grant to be a truancy and drop-out prevention program. The idea was to identify the kids who could not make it in a traditional classroom environment and offer them a viable academic alternative.

We achieved funding from the federal government for one of the first law-enforcement-initiated alternative high schools in the country. Once that was accomplished, I turned the project over to the school district, and they put everything together.

What the school district achieved in building this alternative night school was nothing less than spectacular. Since then, more districts have funded alternative schools of their own. The program is called Excel: Learning For Life. I still sit on the board of directors and speak at commencements for the program. Privately, my wife and I have created two scholarships directed toward kids similar to the ones on these pages.

Britney graduated that first year. Over the past ten years, we've given diplomas to more than a thousand kids like her. I think of that now and then. That's over a thousand times we've helped kids beat the odds.

CHAPTER 14

Artifacts of Suburban Youth

My office in the high school was off the main hallway, directly adjacent to the school's main staircase. It was moved here because of its central location, a deterrent to bad behavior.

Actually a suite of offices enclosed in a windowed cocoon, my office gave me a bird's eye view of the chaos that happened throughout the day as hundreds of people came and went, up and down, this way and that. People could see in and I could see out. But still I needed better surveillance.

Unbeknownst to anyone, I placed a very small nanny-cam inside a rabbit two students had given me after returning from minor surgery. The big, stuffed, pink and blue rabbit, with giant ears, bucked teeth, and large cotton-ball tail watched the rest of the office, particularly the locked file cabinet where I kept my artifacts. The rabbit became my gate-keeper, allowing me to monitor the office remotely, even from home.

But before I tell you about my vault containing mysterious and illegal things, let me tell you more about the rabbit.

Let me introduce you to two of my most beloved characters, Annie and Veronica. They were seniors, always together, co-conspirators, co-defendants, and self-professed Wiccans—as in Witches. I would call them crunchy-granola earth babies.

They would constantly invade my office and talk about anything and everything freely, without restraint, like I wasn't even there. I practiced selective hearing with them because they had no filter, their conversations often inappropriate and a little too personal. But they never seemed to care.

Shortly after I returned to school following one of my surgeries, they brought me a big, fluffy, stuffed rabbit. They named it Little Jackie, after me—endearing, right? We found a home for Little Jackie on the windowsill. One day, they told me that Little Jackie was feeling sick and they thought he had worms. Under Little Jackie's bum, I discovered gummy worms, scattered everywhere.

On Halloween, Jackie was transformed into what they called a Wicked Wiccan, riding a small broom. At Thanksgiving, Jackie became an Indian, feathered headdress and all.

They were great kids. They had a good sense of humor and a good sense of themselves. They'd be in college now. I pity their boyfriends. It's difficult to date, or marry, a girl smarter than you, as I can attest.

They never got into any trouble with me, because in my eyes they could do no wrong. They were as close to normal as any kid I ever dealt with. We were friends and I miss their company.

So, thanks to Annie and Veronica, Little Jackie sat on the windowsill, his mini camera silently watching the goings-on in my office. But other than seeing who was drinking all my coffee, the nanny-cam didn't uncover any secrets, clandestine meetings, or unauthorized access to my desk or vault. I wasn't spying on anyone, just researching new surveillance equipment.

As a self-proclaimed archeologist of urban youth, I collected all kinds of artifacts at the high school and locked them in my file cabinet away from their owners and any other prying eyes.

My collection was impressive. It was also damning if I needed leverage to correct the behavior of some of my pet projects, the ones who inhabited the Zoo. Most of my collectibles were strictly banned from school, the majority of them illegal to boot. My brilliant miscreants' only mistake was believing they could pull the wool over my eyes. I was way too old school to be duped by these Knuckleheads. But I didn't always play fair, and I didn't lose often. I had snitches, and snitches liked hamburgers and an office to hide in when they were bored or too anxious to sit still in class. Tit for tat. Quid quo pro.

Through the years, my collection grew exponentially. It included bullets and shell casings, knives of every size and sharpness, brass knuckles, box cutters, switch blades, a couple of machetes, a miniature cannon, paint-ball guns that looked too real, handcuffs, and throwing stars—the kind that, if thrown correctly, would stick deeply into the intended victim. And no artifact collection is complete without handmade spears. Mine included some that were crafted with real Indian arrowheads. Nothing like taking advantage of our natural resources. There was even a Civil War sword, which is now at my house. The kids brought these things to school for protection, but also to show off. Although I usually carried a little metal detector and a breathalyzer in my pocket, they didn't always reveal the truth. More often than not, I had no idea what these kids had in their backpacks.

Students weren't supposed to be inside an SRO's office, but that didn't stop them. They all knew the rules, yet continued to use my office as their own private lounge.

I had any number of reasons to lock them out. I had extra bulletproof vests in there in case there was a shooting and I needed to protect a wounded kid. I had weapons, even though they were stored dismantled. Police officers are trained to put them back together in the dark or in the rain.

There were a lot of things that, in the wrong hands, could do some real damage—not to mention my computer. It was tied into all of the national crime computer networks. I could find anything about anybody. It was password protected, but that does little to stop hackers these days.

One day, a student by the name of Jerome got his opportunity. The kid was a practical joker and didn't understand what was appropriate and what wasn't.

Although I usually kept my office locked, I was in and out frequently that day. Jerome came through with the head of guidance, heading back into the suite of offices. When I came back to my office, he was the last thing on my mind. I glanced at my desk to find a grenade sitting on top of it. Even though I felt a surge of doom and adrenaline, something in my head said it wasn't real. I picked up. Yes, it had been a grenade once. Now it was a paperweight, hollowed out but still looking very much like the real thing.

Jerome, I thought. *You Knucklehead.* It would send other police officers into a tailspin.

I called him in at once. "Where the hell did you get this thing?" I demanded.

"Home." He shrugged. "It's my dad's."

I picked it up again. "You're lucky I was the one who found it. If it was any other police officer, you'd probably be in jail."

His smirk looked less certain. "Come on, Officer Hobson. Can't you take a joke?"

"This *joke* is called planting a hoax device. It's a federal offense."

"Could I have it back?"

He reached out for it but I pulled it away from him.

"You should have thought about that before you acted like a Knucklehead."

"Please, Officer Hobson. Give it to me."

I shook my head. "I own it. It's mine."

"But Officer…"

"See you later, Jerome. Stay out of trouble."

While I don't know what Jerome learned from that little encounter, I learned to never be surprised by what showed up on my desk.

I didn't collect only weapons. My assortment boasted flasks made of silver, copper, and even real gold. It contained an awesome variety of pipes and bongs, hypodermic needles, masks, pot grinders, and every conceivable kind of drug paraphernalia, including cigarette lighters of every type, make, and style. I had prescription bottles full and empty, the names and types scraped off, of course.

We would bring the dogs into the school on a regular basis. These dogs were so good they could pick up the scent of marijuana as well as certain chemical bonding agents found in prescription medications.

To the students, it was a game. Get caught with under an ounce of marijuana and you paid a hundred-dollar fine. However, get caught with *any* amount of marijuana inside a school and you were looking at expulsion or even jail time.

Instead of doing a criminal record, I would see that the offender got community service and had to take a course, often from me, on drug abuse. I sorted out the drugs and destroyed most of them. The others I saved for when I spoke to schools in the district, using the drugs I had confiscated as tools to show the kids what they looked like as I explained the effects of them.

My wife, Nancy, a supervisor in the drug control unit for the state department of public health, investigates health care professionals with drug problems, who divert drugs from their patients. She was often assigned to work in tandem with federal task forces, answering directly to the U.S. Attorney. On occasion, she would bring some of her team into the school, and even though she was there as a visitor, her presence sent a simple message to the kids: *We can get the DEA in here in a heartbeat.* A not so idle threat.

Open that treasure trove in my office and you'd find recovered jewelry and laptops, cell phones, condoms, a wide collection of very colorful and informative porn material, and sex toys (I'll spare you the details). There were letters professing love, hate, murder, and bomb threats. And there were articles of clothing, bandanas depicting our fake gangs (the Crips and the Bloods), jockstraps, and girls' underwear. In any given school year, I might collect bottles of Vitamin Water filled with all kinds of alcohol (Captain Morgan was my favorite), empty gun holsters, mace, pepper spray, and an array of filed-down toothbrushes and letter openers. These kids watched way too many prison movies.

I had hundreds of dollars of counterfeit money that were made on laser printers and passed at the bookstore and the cafeteria. In a busy lunch line with things happening so quickly, it was difficult to spot even bad counterfeit bills.

I knew, though, when the fake bills were flying. Kids are always talking about things, especially the snitch kids. They couldn't keep their mouths shut. After we had a lot of incidents with that, I had an assembly with all of the kids by grade level.

"Passing those fake bills is a federal crime," I told them. "You'll be kicked out of school. And if you're doing it over the price of a hamburger, you're crazy. How stupid would you look if you went to jail over a hamburger?"

I tried to create an atmosphere of collective responsibility and guilt. Then I would call down the guilty parties to my office and give them enough of a talking-to that they knew if they didn't knock it off, they were gone. Before long, the Great Counterfeit Caper ended—for that term at least.

If I had wanted to, I could have made their lives difficult for a while. But teachable moments are few and far between.

CHAPTER 15

Sailing with Captain Morgan

Since the beginning of time, high school students at some point dance with the devil and experiment with alcohol. The ever-present forbidden fruit can be the focal point of an afternoon get-together or the source of anticipation for a weekend blowout.

When I was young, beer was king. We'd plead with an older brother to buy it for us. In desperate times, we'd hang out in front of a liquor store, called a *packy* in Boston, and beg strangers to do the dirty work.

On a quiet day while roaming the halls, I was called on my radio to meet up with the nurse. Finding Maria, she told me that a boy had been throwing up and dry-heaving on-and-off all morning. As we entered his classroom, I saw the Knucklehead on his hands and knees, heaving and missing the trash can with his eruption.

His name was Liam. I knew him as a fringe kid who usually behaved and kept to himself.

"Liam, my man, what's your malfunction?" I asked.

He looked at me through watery eyes, his nose bleeding profusely. I handed him my handkerchief so he could wipe the blood off his face. *Only a bloody nose,* I thought, *but with a familiar smell.*

Blood smells like copper. Add alcohol to it and it smells like a cross between an orange and ammonia. A familiar smell, or at least familiar to police officers. Maria was concerned and we talked about calling for an ambulance. We also discussed the possible spread of germs and handling worried parents as the stress and tension mounted. I asked Maria to join me in the hall for a chat. "Why weren't you called earlier when Liam first threw up?"

"My understanding is that Liam said he was okay and didn't want to leave class," Maria said.

Thinking out loud, I said to Maria, "I smelled what I'm sure is alcohol on his breathe and I got a better whiff off his bloody nose. Liam's wasted and so shitfaced he can't hit the waste basket."

"Drunk? You sure?"

"Yah, I'm sure. If I had to guess he drank before class and felt sick a short time later. Blood alcohol can increase, decrease, or level off at different rates, depending on body weight, proximity to your last meal, or drinking tolerance. I don't think Liam's an experienced drinker," I told the nurse as she pushed a wheel chair into the class to scoop up our sick and wild-eyed friend.

"Think I ought to go back and bring a stretcher?"

"No, let's hoist him up and take him to your office. We'll check him out away from all these prying eyes."

We wheeled Liam away, the reeking stench of alcohol and partially digested food following us like a dark cloud.

We were almost into the elevator when a teacher yelled, "Maria, come quick!"

A girl had fainted in the hall. With her back to her locker, she'd lost gravity and, like a melting snowman, had slid down into a sitting position. Liz was a good kid. I knew her parents. She was drifting in and out of a few peer groups, but was generally liked by all. We bent down, shook her, snapped our fingers in front of her face, but the young girl didn't respond.

"She's out," I said. "Snoring easily, but definitely out."

Maria took her blood pressure. It was normal, her other vital signs acceptable. "We'll need a stretcher for her," she said.

I called an ambulance. Then my eyes scanned the student landscape of the classroom. I was looking for a furtive movement, in poker it's called a tell. It's like a subtle nervous tick that betrays a straight face. As I scanned the room I made eye contact with a few of my usual suspects. Then I saw it. My man Ricky Slap, a long time Knucklehead, had broken his eye contact with me— a feeble attempt to look cool, but to me he looked guilty, or at least appeared to have a guilty conscious.

I brought Ricky into the hallway. This kid owed me big time. In middle school, he would fight anyone at the drop of a dime if someone looked at him the wrong way or if he was simply bored. Hell, he had even punched me a few times. He was a Knucklehead personified, but I liked him and I was doing my best to help him adjust to high school. He was one of my works in progress.

"Who has the booze, Slap?"

"I have no idea, Officer Hobson."

"Sla—ppy," I whispered, drawing out the two syllables in his name. "Don't fuck with me, not right now. I'm not playing."

A teacher was at my shoulder as the stretcher arrived. "Jack, why do you call Ricky, Slappy?" she asked.

"Oh, he's been on my radar since middle school. I think he holds the all-time record for detention hours served. I used to tell him if he kept fighting he'd become slap-happy like a boxer with brain damage. I started by calling him just *slap*, but when other kids called him that name, he'd slap them, so, slap-happy became Slappy. Inside joke between us."

"Oh, that's just awesome."

"Yeah, right," I said, making eye contact with Ricky. He knew what I was talking about.

As we loaded Liz onto the stretcher, I noticed the hall had been cleared. The principal had called for a stay-in-place, a soft lockdown, where everyone was required to stay in their classrooms. There was no threat to the school, but we needed room for clear transport.

I found a flask in Liam's locker. It looked expensive and old, his grandfather's perhaps. Too nice to have been bought at a yard sale or flea market. It was filled with whiskey, though I couldn't place the brand, maybe Jameson's Irish whiskey, potent stuff. Also, I found vitamin bottles full of liquid. Dark rum, Captain Morgan's maybe.

"Slappy, my man," I said, "is anyone else involved? Anyone going to heave all over themselves and pass out?" I got two names and another flask. This one was gold or gold-plated with whiskey inside. Their plans were thwarted before any more damage could be done.

Two flasks—good haul.

Liz was taken to the hospital. The paramedics checked out Liam and he was released to his parents. The two other boys were sent home, suspended. The situation was handled and the crisis averted, all wrapped up with a neat little bow by nine-thirty in the morning.

I let them off light, perhaps too light by some people's standards, but I held the leverage of evidence ready, should something happen again.

CHAPTER 16

Shuriken Throwing Star

Out of the blue one morning, a physical education teacher called and asked if I could come to the gym—the varsity football team's locker room, specifically.

"What's up?" I asked.

"Jack, this is something you have to see to believe."

When I arrived in the gymnasium, I was met by a coach who directed my attention to two boys sequestered in his office. "What did they do?" I asked.

"Follow me," he said.

The locker room was quiet and empty, but reeking of various odors: liniments, chlorine, rubber, sweat, and damp. That ageless, ever-present locker room aroma. He led me to a bank of lockers that appeared severely damaged.

"Looks like someone took a can opener to 'em," I said. "What happened?"

"Follow me," he said with a labored breath

I did until we stood in front of another bank of lockers. Impaled in one was a Japanese throwing star, a ninja weapon if you prefer.

"A Shuriken throwing star," I said.

"You ought to know, Jack."

"No shit," I said. "The boys? This their handy work?"

"Oh yeah," the coach said.

"How did you catch them?" I asked.

"I was in my office and I heard a strange sound, couldn't place it, then I heard yelling. No one's supposed to be in the locker during that time."

"So you went in and found those two dudes."

"Yeah, they were trying to pull that thing out of the metal."

I gripped the star, working on it until finally it pulled free from the metal. "Look at how it's damn near fused in here. Imagine," I said, "what this thing would do to a body, flesh and blood."

"That would suck," said the coach.

The boys were on the football team, one a junior, the other a freshman. Both were popular and considered to be good kids. But that day's antics would be expensive, the cost to be measured in the consequences. I didn't really question them as part of an investigation, but I wanted to know what had possessed them to do something so stupid.

And to add insult to injury, they had pulled out the star a couple of times, causing damage to three lockers. Here's the thing: someone would have to pay for the damage. I could have them suspended and most likely have them banned from playing sports. I could charge them with malicious destruction of property, and I could pile on a possession of a dangerous weapon charge. I didn't.

We, the coach and I, the parents of the accused, the athletic director, and Big Nick, decided that the two miscreants would be suspended for 7 days and could not play football for the rest of the season. In addition, they had to write a ten-page essay about respect and integrity and how their stupid decisions affected the school. Although I am the law enforcement representative for the district, I can yield to the principal regarding the filing of charges and the extent of an investigation. In other words, if the school wants my involvement and I proceed with a criminal investigation, more specifically if I scrutinize the facts in relation to delinquency guidelines, then it's in for a penny, in for a pound and discretion on my part, ends. As these students learned very quickly, retribution and paying the price is not always monetary, sometimes money can't make things right. Those stars are lethal and deadly, not intended to be in the hands of anyone, really, especially not a couple of Knuckleheads.

That's how I came into possession of my throwing star. I brought it home, gripped it by the top prong, and threw it like I was skimming a rock on water. It flew like a Frisbee and hooked abruptly off course, its flight like a boomerang, and embedded itself into my neighbor's fence, deep into the plastic.

Who's the Knucklehead now?

CHAPTER 17

Mario: Two Weapons Too Many.

A t the high school, the juniors had their own parking lot, far away from the main building and out of the reach of video surveillance. The junior parking lot, some 300 yards away from the school and far away from my sight-line and that of the big brother surveillance cameras, was a harbor for Knucklehead behavior. It's so far away, that before I could respond or before the school could be notified of a problem, the suspects were usually long gone.

It was like a pirate's haven—a place where kids would fight, break into and damage each other's cars, steal things, spray paint penises, obscenities, and other vulgar messages on car hoods, windows, dumpsters, and the pavement. It was a place to hang out, smoke, and talk between classes. And it was never a surprise to me that kids who were skipping school would eventually end up in the lot, thinking they could hide in plain sight.

Not so much.

Throughout the years, that parking lot had been the arena for many fights, disturbances, and other encounters.

One sunny peaceful day, I was beeped with a 911 message to call the front office. As I was outside walking,

I called on my cell. They told me I was needed immediately in the juniors' parking lot.

The only information I received was sketchy, something about an attack. Students were hurt and a weapon had been used.

"What kind of weapon," I asked.

"A sword."

"A sword?" I called my station for a back-up patrolman.

As I exited my cruiser, I observed several things happening at the same time. It's called the whole view, processing multiple pieces of information simultaneously. I saw a boy on the ground, surrounded by other students. I saw a car parked perpendicular to the parking space with its driver door open. I saw a person in the distance, running, possibly running away. Two other boys were yelling. A couple of girls were crying.

I approached the crowd. "Who's hurt?" I asked, looking around, focusing on everyone and everything.

"Paul is," a boy piped up. "He got punched and kicked in the head while he was on the ground."

"Anyone else?"

"Nope."

I checked Paul out. EMS was on the way. Other police officers had arrived. I was still confused about the sword report, but an assessment of the scene told me that no active threat was present.

I separated the witnesses. "Who punched and kicked Paul?"

"Kid called Mario." This came from Hunter, a senior I recognized.

"Say no more. I know him well."

That August, before the start of the school year, I was on regular patrol and got dispatched to a neighborhood dispute. Someone had broken a bay window in the front of the caller's house and the hood of his car and his mailbox were splattered with blue paint.

"The kid next door, Mario, has a paintball gun and he goes around shooting it at anything and everything."

"Paintballs don't break windows. I'll bet he's freezing them." I had seen that before. It was somewhat of a fad, or maybe a phase that boys go through at a certain age. They like to play with guns. In my day, our paintball equivalent weapon was an air gun. We would fill the barrel with mud and fire the slush at anyone or anything.

When I went to Mario's house, his father opened the door. I asked for Mario and had him bring out his paintball gun. It was CO_2 powered and looked like an assault rifle. As I suspected, Mario was freezing the paintballs. So when he loaded them into the gun, it was like he was shooting marbles.

Mario's dad had paid restitution for the neighbor s damaged property—repainting the car alone cost about a grand. I took the paintball gun with dad's blessing.

I asked Hunter where Mario was.

"He took off that way."

He pointed in the direction I had seen the kid running earlier. In the distance, the kid had stopped for a second, before he began running again.

"From the beginning, Hunter, what happened?" I said.

"Paul and Mario were at each other all day at school," he said. "Text messages, yelling in the halls, friends of each bumping and posturing. Paul hooked up with Mario's girlfriend, Brenda."

"Hooked up? Had sex?"

"Yeah, I think so." Hunter blushed. "Mario was talking about it."

"How did Mario find out?"

"How does anybody find out anything?" He paused as if I'd asked a dumb question. "Facebook," he said.

"What's this shit about a sword?"

"Mario said he had one and Paul was gonna be his victim."

"What did he actually say?"

"He said he was gonna chop his balls off."

Ouch, I thought. "Did anyone see a sword?"

"No, he keeps it in his car."

"Have you seen it, does he ever take it out to show it off or brag about it?" I asked trying to align the charges in my head if I had to file an arrest report. "Where's his car?"

Hunter looked back toward the parking lot. "Right there," he said. "The one with the door open. He heard your siren and split, running that way."

Mario was no rocket scientist. He must have been freaked.

I walked across the lot and searched the car while the other police officers were taking statements. Between the front seat and console, I found a machete knife wedged under the arm rest. Its blade looked to be about fourteen inches long, very sharp, with a silver duct-taped handle. Other than a few burnt roaches in the ashtray, I found no other weapons. I had his car towed, another expense for his parents as they would have to pay to claim it.

That's how I got my machete. Mario's dad showed up at the police station with Mario in tow and asked for me. I took a statement from Mario and he was released back into his father's custody. There would be a subsequent court appearance on charges of assault with a dangerous weapon and possession of same, to wit: a machete.

On the school end, Mario went through all the rings and hoops that constitute academic and administrative due process. Mario was suspended until his arraignment. Until the juvenile court made a decision, Mario was a man without a school.

CHAPTER 18

You Gotta Know When To Fold Them

The three to six hours after classes end offer a window of time where many kids get into trouble. Unsupervised, they mingle in places they feel no one will be watching. The more the police get involved, the farther into the shadows they wander. The last thing a cop wants to do is troll for teens, moving them away from doorways and empty buildings by handing them a no-trespass order.

One of the grants I wrote while going through my doctoral program was a twenty-thousand dollar endowment for a youth center, a place these wandering kids could hang out during those vulnerable hours.

"I believe we can reduce juvenile crime if we start up a youth center," I said to anyone who'd listen.

"Anyplace you try to put it will be too expensive," they'd argue.

I mentioned an old school building that had stood vacant since it was shut down. "Its basement would be perfect," I said.

"What about stuff like furniture?"

"I can get it donated." I smiled. "Even some pinball machines and jukeboxes."

"Who's going to run it?"

"Me," I said, "and my staff will be made up of other volunteer police officers."

We got the grant and I was the director. There was no problem getting other officers to volunteer. The only hitch here was officers were paid for their time. Nothing is free.

Soon, people were talking about how good it was for the town.

I took a look at all of the kids in detention and those who were getting suspended for not trying to keep up with their assignments. "As an alternative to this negative behavior," I said to the superintendent, "let's find out where they need help the most, what subjects are bogging them down, and we'll get college kids to tutor them."

The superintendent seemed enthusiastic. "I know the colleges have intern programs," he said. "They might be valuable to this type of program."

"At our youth center," I put in quickly, before his interest waned.

We were on our way. College students, not far removed from the high school-aged youths, would arrive at the center and oversee teaching chores for the first hour. That was the tradeoff. Study with your tutor for an hour then hang out together for the second hour. It became an alternative program. Many kids signed up and it worked out very well.

One day, while visiting the center, I spotted two high school boys playing dice against the wall, like the sidewalk craps game I had played myself as a kid. Or so I thought. Soon I realized they weren't just competing for fun, they were playing for money.

"I don't mind if you play a dice game," I told them. "But no money is going to be exchanged." Curious about the two high rollers, I went to their guidance counselor. "How are these two boys doing in school?"

She looked up their grades. No surprise, they were both deficient in math, one to a great degree, the other not so bad.

"How about you give them to me at the youth center?" I suggested.

The college students who tried to help them soon told me the boys refused to listen. It became clear they needed motivation to learn math.

That motivation had been right in front of my eyes.

"Can you approach math as odds and percentages?" I asked one college tutor.

She seemed interested. "In what way?"

"They like to play dice," I said.

She thought for a moment. "I'll need some help."

"That's where I come in," I said.

It wasn't too long before the two became more interested in math. Nothing very dramatic, but we did notice some improvement in school.

છૂગ્છૂગ

Getting into these kids' heads required different approaches. I liked the element of surprise, interrogating them on Mondays, when the weekend was still in their thoughts.

"So how did you spend your weekend?" I asked a student one Monday, before he'd gotten his school legs. Sure enough, this got me some interesting information, a bit of knowledge I hadn't expected.

"Playing poker," he said.

"Where?"

"Basement at my house."

"Yeah?" I almost yelled at him. "What kind of poker?"

"S—strip p—poker," he sputtered, "with some girls."

"Yeah, right, you guys couldn't get a girl to give you the right time," I said, shaking my head.

I took it with a grain of salt at first, but then playing cards started showing up the way bandanas had during the gang period. Thinking I'd better nip it in the bud, I alerted the principal. "Might not be a big problem," I informed her, "but we've got to get the cards out of the school."

We decided that every home room teacher would explain that cards were no longer allowed, that gambling was as bad as drugs. So the cards began to disappear.

Then dice started showing up. I was always willing to overlook minor bad behavior, especially if I could gain knowledge of major trouble through snitches. Leverage is like currency with these kids.

One of the boys, whom I had confiscated dice from, tried to gain points by telling me about football cards. This really piqued my interest. I wasn't really worried about dice, but football cards were on a whole different level.

Football cards were part of a larger gambling issue. They required a puppet master, and there was no telling how far up the chain we'd have to go to find him.

Football cards go back quite a few years. Originally, they were little more than a list of the upcoming college games. Soon professional games were added. Each match up gave the point spread between favorites and underdogs. For instance, Michigan might be listed as a three point favorite over Notre Dame. Ties, called pushes, were not counted. Those betting would have to add a ten percent *vig*, an up-front payment similar to interest, on all losing bets. Called "the juice" on the street, this made up the profit the bookies hoped to gain. Present day football cards reflected the "action" wagered in casinos in Las Vegas and were gaining a frenzied measure of popularity.

It wasn't long before I began to hear about cards being circulated. Kids were bragging about winning. Others were despondent when they lost. I had to discover just how prevalent the cards were and who was distributing them. We had to consider the possibility that kids in the high school might be runners for mid-level or big-time bookies.

At the youth center, one of the kids was talking about filling out a card.

I cornered him. "Who gave you the card?"

"Don't know."

Here we go again, I thought. "Don't give me that shit."

"A guy named Josh," he finally confessed. "I think he might have given me one."

A kid named Josh. Trouble seemed to be his middle name. His father was in prison and his mother was doing the best she could to hold the family together. Josh wasn't making it easy for her. He seemed to be seeking an identity, unable to find one that fit.

"Have you seen the cards?" I asked the kid.

"No, but everybody knows that they're doing it."

I didn't go right after Josh. I needed some evidence, a cause to search him. I didn't know how I was going to proceed and then, as it often happened, a fight broke out between Josh and another boy that proved to be telling. I broke it up, took them to the nurse for a quick patch up, then marched them into the principal's office.

"I was protecting my friend from Josh," the boy said.

"What was Josh after?" I asked.

"He was collecting money from a football card bet."

There it was—the cause I needed to search him.

I suggested both boys get back to class and told the principal I'd work on investigating the situation. I decided to put together a sting operation.

I had a kid who was stealing backpacks from the locker room and had decided to arrest him, moving toward getting him suspended, but I knew he was an acquaintance of Josh's. And I was sure the kid would do anything to stay in school, to keep his father from going to jail for murdering him. Two birds with one stone was how I looked at it.

Josh was bringing the cards to school. They were unique, and it was easy to see they were straight out of Las Vegas's morning line. The Las Vegas line or odds was calculated using a bunch of different variables depending on the sport. But betting the line, for those of us who have and lost, is taking a chance on a future bet, one a couple of days away. It's called a logic model in the stock market—a best guess on future losses and gains. Winnings were paid and losses collected. Those were the rules. Period. This wasn't your average high school adventure by any stretch of the imagination.

Because Josh was dealing football cards, that put him in a league beyond my jurisdiction. So before I passed the investigation forward, I needed proof, not necessarily evidence, but probable cause.

I fixed the school cameras to watch the hall where Josh's locker was located. After a few weeks, the computerized camera footage showed Josh at his open locker with another kid, Josh clearly handing something over to his visitor. From my viewpoint, it looked like a football card, but I wasn't sure.

The next day, I talked to the principal. "I can't search Josh's locker without cause," I said, "but you can." When the principal opened Josh's locker, I felt a pang of sorrow. I immediately found five cards. Though unmarked, they were still bad news. Mere possession of them was against the law, not to mention against school rules, codes of conduct, and policies. If I didn't get him, the school would.

We took Josh out of class and called his mother. When she came, I advised him of his rights, the football cards in my hands.

"I found them," Josh said, acting cocky. "I don't know what you're talking about."

I moved him outside where I could have a word with him in private. "Cut the shit," I said in my best cop whisper. "I can arrest you right now for gambling on school property, and I've been told that you've threatened students who lost money to pay up or else. Am I right?" I said as my eyes focused intently on his. "You know, Josh, it's a felony to gamble and the statue has a lot of sub-sections. Believe me, you don't want me to starting writing."

He looked distressed, but said nothing. I searched my memory for crimes associated with gambling, crimes that are peripheral and can be added to a gambling offense as supplementary.

"There are state statutes that deal with collecting money lost through gambling, like assault and battery and threatening someone with bodily harm in order to collect a debt." I held his stare until he blinked. "If I charge you for any of those," I said, "you'll be kicked out of school for good."

He looked at his feet then toward his mother, sitting there in the open room with the principal. "Yeah, I had them."

"Any money exchange hands?" I asked.

"Not really."

"What do you mean?"

"A couple of dollars here and there."

I told the principal I needed more time with him. "Get him back in school tomorrow," I said.

In the meantime, I talked to SROs in other schools. One of them a couple of towns over had the same problem.

When Josh came in the next day, I had a detective with me, who had a totally different style of interrogation than I did. Right to the point was his manner, right to the law.

Josh cracked. "All right," he said in a defeated tone. "I sold some cards to some kids."

"Where are you getting the cards?" the detective asked.

"This guy in another town," Josh mumbled. "I go every Friday and turn in the money."

"And?"

"He gives me cards for the next week."

Once the tough guy, Josh was now the bait. I turned the investigation over to detectives who were already handling this gambling syndicate case. We wanted to know where they were doing business and how many kids like Josh were acting as runners for them in other schools. The investigation took a while. Josh was treated as a CI, confidential informant. *TV stuff,* I told myself, all done with his mother's blessing. With Mom's okay, Josh became a regular CI for the detectives.

Half of the kids involved gave me statements and I turned my reports over to the task force. After six or eight months, they arrested bookies a couple of towns over. Turned out, there were several high schools where kids were running football cards.

Josh was exonerated because I wasn't going to muddy the waters of the investigation by arresting him. His cooperation, along with the information I'd obtained from other schools, helped the department make some arrests.

Josh ended up providing the break the task force needed. They followed up with some solid cases against the bookies and were able to stop the football card gambling.

We had another challenge ahead of us, however. Where you find gambling, you find evidence of other, sometimes unbelievable, realities. In this case, gangs.

CHAPTER 19

The Crips, the Pond Scum Boys,
and the Get Money Goons

B andanas. Each day we noticed more and more of them. Solid blue, they hung out of back left pockets and were tied tightly around left knees. I probably wouldn't have given them a second thought, except there were so many of them. Like an infestation of bad fashion, these blue bandanas were displayed everywhere.

At first, some of us thought this was some kind of school wide fashion statement. Then came the blue hats, tilted to the left—L.A. Dodgers hats, right here in the heart of the Red Sox nation.

Now, I was interested.

More of a curiosity than an issue at that point, the problem had me walking the halls, asking kids politely to take off their hats. "No hats inside the school," I said to rule breakers. "It's been a school policy since the beginning."

Then came the defiance, the cocky reactions, always in a rebellious tone. "I'm representing, cuzz."

"What? Who?" I demanded of one kid. "Take that hat off. Are you hard of hearing?"

"Nope," the culprit said as he walked away.

Yeah, I knew this kid, a real wise-ass. "Stop, Jason. Don't make me ask you twice, my friend." I squared off in front of him. "What's with the bandanas and hats?"

"We represent the Crips," he said.

"The Crips?" I took the hat off his head and watched his whole body tense. "Cut the shit," I told him in an even voice. "And keep it off while you're inside."

I soon learned this type of encounter was being experienced daily by teachers and other staff. This sort of student revolt was just the first shot across the bow. The next couple of days would not only test my patience, it would show me how stubborn, silly, and absurd teenagers can be when they feel they've taken a noble stand.

As this gang nonsense gained traction at the high school, I was called over to the middle school directly across the street from us. The principal, Paul, was a friend of mine and he wanted to show me some graffiti sprayed on the side of one of their dumpsters.

He led me around the back of the school and pointed to the letters *PSB* spray-painted rather artistically on a dumpster in purple and red. "Jack," he said, "what does it mean?"

I cocked my head and gave it my full attention. "I got nothin'."

Jake, a janitor, joined us. "Come look at this one," he said.

On the side of the field house were the letters *GMG*. Both he and Paul gave me a look that said, *You're the cop, what's going on here?*

"No clue," I said. "Let me see what I can dig up."

Jake had been around a long time. A good guy, he took a lot of pride in his work. I knew he wanted the graffiti gone immediately.

"Leave it for a couple of days," I told him. "If we take it down too soon, they might see it as a challenge."

A couple of days before, while I was out fishing, I'd picked up one of my regular stragglers, a kid named Sean. He reeked of pot, but I only found half a cigarette and a lighter when I searched him. I'd told him to get into my vehicle and dropped him off at school. "Get your ass up to the Zoo," I instructed him.

He now owed me about a thousand favors.

When I returned from my trip to the middle school, I called the Zoo and asked if Sean could be sent to my office. I could hear the jeers and shouts from the classroom as the teacher sent him my way.

Sean had no idea what the shortest distance between two points was. A five-minute trip could take him a wandering half hour. So I decided to meet him halfway.

"What did I do now, Officer Hobson?" he asked at once.

"Guilty conscience, Sean?"

"What?"

"Never mind." I walked him over against the wall of lockers. "Okay, here it is. Tell me about all this gang crap and the paint on the middle school."

"I don't—"

"Cut the shit, Sean," I demanded. "Just spill it."

"Okay," he said in a weak voice. "But it's stupid."

What wasn't stupid around here? I thought. "I'm listening, Sean. What does *PSB* mean?"

"Pond Scum Boys," he said, only half smiling, like he knew he could be in big trouble with me and maybe a lot of other people. "It's a made-up gang name."

"Okay. Now, how about *GMG*?"

At that, he boldly laughed out loud. I was trying hard not to join him.

"That stands for the Get Money Goons," he explained.

"Get Money *what*?" I said.

"G—goons, you know like the m—movie, *Goonies*," he said, stammering a bit.

"Whatever. Another made-up name?"

"Yeah, but why me, Officer Hobson?" He was no longer laughing. "If they know I'm talking to you," he said in a shaky voice, "I'm toast, man."

"I think you better take a deep breath," I said. "And start from the beginning."

He shivered, as if a cold draft had hit him. "It's t— this g—guy, P-Dog, and his friends," he sputtered. "They think they're real gangsters. They have meetings, and I've heard they have weapons and shit." He looked at me. "You've seen all the hats and the scarves?"

"The bandanas?"

"Yeah, whatever."

"Okay, Sean," I said. "Go back to class. Don't worry, your name won't ever come up."

I arranged for a meeting with the principals, other police officers, selected teachers, and counselors to talk about this small but growing issue. After the gathering, I met with another police officer and told him I had an idea.

The following day, with my new partner present, I called a kid, named Tony, into my office but everyone knew him as P-Dog.

P-Dog was a tough kid on the outside. His mother struggled with his attitude and defiance. His father, a motorcycle type, was in jail for a gang-related bust. Too many kids had fathers in jail, I thought.

"All right, Mr. P," I said, after he sat down, "this Crip shit needs to be kept out of the school, and that's not a request."

He gave us a long look. "Aren't you going to read me my rights or something?"

"This isn't a game, P-Dog," I told him "What does P-dog even mean, Tony," I asked.

"It was supposed to be T-dog, for top dog, the boss, but some idiots started calling me P-dog and it stuck."

"Some idiots, huh? They'll mess you up. Can't live with them, can't have a gang without them," I said a little too sarcastically. "Parents are worried, kids are being kept home from school, and it's all because of rumors about this gang shit."

"They're not rumors. It's our lifestyle," he said.

"Okay, tough guy, let's make a little wager. Here's two ten-dollar bills." I placed the bills in front of him. "Tell me how the Crips got their name and their reputation. You do, and the money's yours."

"It's a West Coast thing," P-Dog said. "They conquered other gangs and took their turf. Now they run things."

"Just like that? That sounds way too easy. They just conquered everyone and took over. I don't think so," I taunted. "That's it? That's all you got?" I began pacing in front of him. "This is the East Coast, remember? We have some very bad-ass Boston gangs, you know?"

"They're all pussies!"

"So you don't know? And all these cryptic symbols and finger signs are nothing more than Mr. Spock telling us to live long and to prosper?" I came to a stop and relaxed. This kid needed some education.

"Let me tell you about your boys, your tough-guy Crips," I said. "Back in the 1970s, a gang was formed in east L.A. One of the first. They called themselves the Avenues, because that's what they controlled. As you said, it was their turf. Then another group organized and wanted to align themselves with the Avenues. They called themselves the Baby Avenues."

I walked over to my partner, a big guy looming in his uniform, all his fire power and gear fitting him snugly. When I turned back to P-dog, he'd slouched down in his chair.

"And they called their turf their crib. So, here's the best part. These Baby Avenues, who, by the way, wore bandanas and carried canes, decided that they would make a name for themselves, you know, enhance their street rep. So they robbed a bunch of old women. *Old women*, Tony. Tough guys, right? When the police asked the women for a description, they told the cops that they were jumped by a bunch of cripples. The Cripples became known as the Crips." I stood above him with my arms crossed. "Tell me, P-Dog, who are the pussies now?"

My fellow police officer talked to me later. "Very impressive," he said. "Especially the part where you told him about your own gang."

"We're like a gang, right?"

"Yeah, right, more like an insane clown posse."

Anyhow, about ten of us clowns searched the school, confiscating nearly every bandana, hat, and all those notebooks full of gang symbols. "You should see the shit in these notebooks: skulls, Nazi signs, zombies, and all kinds of other doom and gloom shit. It's a little unnerving," I said.

I didn't need to be told how I'd impressed upon P-Dog not to try me. "We'll get everything you have, P," I let him know. "You hear me? My gang is bigger than yours. Don't—" I warned him. "—and I mean, *don't*— ever test us."

A few mild skirmishes followed, and a couple of defiant holdouts tested our resolve, but in the end, the Crips, like Elvis, had left the building—for now.

Tony's mother became an uneasy ally of mine. Tough on the outside, she admitted that she couldn't get through to this one of her three children. His father had been in and out of jail, and still Tony considered him a role model. His mother told me that his father gave him the top dog handle.

"That's why Joshua thinks gangs are so cool," she told me during one of our informal conferences.

"Some of these youths feel that joining up with an underground group is a noble rite of passage," I said.

Later that same day, I found Tony on campus. "You know," I told him, "we're not in a big city, where you need someone watching your back every minute." I sized him up in my mind and considered the choice he'd made to hang on to his father's influence. "What do you think would've happened, had you been busted for being the boss to a bunch of Knuckleheads?"

He shrugged. "Don't know."

"Well, think about what a few hardened cons in jail would do to a little white kid who thought he was a Crip."

He didn't have an answer for me.

His mother continued to keep after him. I would speak with her cautiously, knowing she'd been caught and trapped big time in the web of the criminal justice system. I was working it, but she was living it. In the end, she finally got to his father and convinced him to tell their son that what he'd been up to wasn't cool. "You don't want to end up like me," his dad finally admitted.

One of the problems tied to gangs is the reaction parents have to any such activity at their kids' school. When rumors of gangs turned to factual evidence, they began to keep their kids home, rather than send them to school. We had a hotline where anyone could phone tips in to us, so we might nip gang activity in the bud. This episode involving Tony set off a rash of texting from parents.

"Why weren't we notified earlier?" many demanded.

We ended up releasing statements to the media, and members of our administration appeared on cable television. "There is no major gang problem," a school representative would explain, "regardless of what you may be hearing."

For the most part, this was true, but we did have a graffiti problem and that brought on more pressure from the citizenry. Their fences, garage doors, and traffic signs were being tagged.

Even though I found that there was very little organization in the bands of taggers, I kept chasing them. Some, it was easy to see, were artists in their own right. Every group had their Rembrandt.

I spoke to the manager of the local hardware store. "You have kids in here buying spray paint cans," I said to him, like it was a statement, not a question.

"All the time," he admitted.

I gave him my card. "When high school-age kids come in to buy spray paint," I said, "give me a call."

He did. I responded in time to catch two kids with their money out, several cans on the counter. When I asked what they needed the paint for, they both played dumb.

"We need it for a job," one finally said.

"What kind of job?

They drew a blank.

"How about I call your parents and we find out?"

I decided to stop their art expression with a warning. "The Pond Scum Gang is known for their tagging," I notified them. "And it's up to me to fix the problem."

They waited, mum and worried. I waved the proprietor over and spoke to all three of them. "Did you know in the Commonwealth of Massachusetts, we have a few misdemeanor crimes that don't have to be committed in the presence of a police officer?" Obviously, they did not or they weren't going to volunteer an answer. "The crimes are graffiti, drunk driving, and gambling," I said. "And we can make an arrest after the fact, even now, right here, starting with you two Knuckleheads."

Sometimes, all you have to do is spread the word.

∽∾∽

Nearing the end of the school year, P-Dog was suspended for eight days. He'd beaten up a kid in the bathroom for making fun of his gang.

Christ, I thought, *here we go again. Does it never end? Is now the time to make that terrible choice of throwing a kid into the criminal justice system?*

Sometimes that was the best thing we could do. And sometimes it was the worst.

In the juvenile system, Tony might end up with an ankle bracelet and be confined to his home after school. Often, I would yield to the kids' parents to make the decision. In this case, I'd talk with his mother. I thought of what might happen. I knew Tony would be defiant. That was a given. Would his mother become afraid of her own son? She was tough, but how tough? Had his father convinced him that following him wasn't the way to go? Would time take the edge off the problem?

A lot of kids seemed to outgrow their bad behavior. Others needed more than any of us could give.

CHAPTER 20

Irish Twins

This isn't a story of another kid gone bad. It's the story of two good kids caught in a criminal situation, one that could have caused them to lose everything.

I had known Rosemary and Sylvia O'Leary from when they were elementary school. They were what we called Irish twins, fourteen years old and born within ten months of each other. Their mother, a nurse, had been a volunteer for school events, and their father worked as a computer analyst. The family lived in a large colonial home on a cul-de-sac in an upper middle-class neighborhood that had once been farmland. The girls were blonde and well liked, with bubbly personalities.

As far as I could tell, everything was fine in their lives.

Then tragedy struck. Their mother was killed by a drunk driver and everything changed. Their father lost his energy, his hope. He started to drink, and even though he had these two beautiful kids to raise, he was kind of neglecting them.

One night, at the local bar, he met Shelly, younger than he, a long-haired brunette, wearing tight jeans and a *come-get-me* look. They started to date, and after a month or so, the father moved Shelly and Monique, her fourteen-year-old daughter, into their home.

Soon, the O'Leary girls were spending time in the school nurse's office, the one place where they could say what was on their minds. Sometimes I was part of these discussions. The girls didn't like Shelly and they liked Monique even less. Something about the situation made me uncomfortable. Just a hunch at first. Still, I didn't like what I was hearing and suspected there might be more going on than anyone knew. But *what*?

I started out by considering the options offered by the Department of Youth Services and the Department of Social Services.

When I was bothered by issues larger than the usual I faced at school, I paced, and my wife, Nancy, noticed. I paced for two nights before she asked me what was wrong.

"Those kids, the O'Learys. They are going to end up going to DSS," I told her. "There is nobody else left. They are going to be taken away from their home."

"Why don't you do what's in your heart?" she asked.

"Because what I want to do in my heart isn't exactly legal."

In my mind, I tried to think about the definition of a conspiracy. I tried to see everything I could be charged with and circumvent it somehow. So if anyone came to me and asked if I told the girls to do what I had in mind, I could say no. Once I'd wrestled with myself; discussed my options with Nancy; and made my plan right, in my own head and heart, I knew I was ready the next time I saw the girls crying at school.

It wasn't long.

"You know," I told them that day. "Gathering evidence, assuming you would want to, takes time. It takes attention to detail, writing down everything, even if it doesn't seem important at the time. Get my drift?"

They nodded, eyes wide. These poor kids had lost their mother—and now, in a way, they were losing their dad, too. Not just to the drinking, but to this woman who seemed to be moving into their territory way too fast.

A week or two later, they were in the nurse's office again, sobbing uncontrollably.

The nurse motioned me in.

"Rosemary," I said, "Sylvia. Calm down and tell me what happened."

"It's their dad," the nurse said. "Shelly called 911 last night. According to her, he was shoving her around and he inappropriately touched her daughter, Monique. The police gave him a restraining order and forced him to move out."

"She won't let us upstairs," Rosemary said through her tears. "We have to stay downstairs where the bedrooms are and watch TV. She says she wants to keep us out of her hair."

"How in the world is that possible?" Sylvia asked through her tears. "How can our dad be kicked out of his own house while Shelly and Monique are taking it over?"

That brought on a new round of sobbing.

"She won't be able to for long," I said. "It's still his home, and it's your home." Again, I felt that warning instinct that there was more to this than met the eye. "I need to check the restraining order warrant and see how long it's in force."

I was going to check more than that.

Usually, we wouldn't want kids in on a discussion of that type, but these girls had been keeping records of what went on in the house, and the facts didn't add up. Their dad hadn't been even been around to do what Shelly and Monique had accused him of.

Shelly knew what she was doing. The order was for two weeks, a long time for these girls to be without their dad. It was also time enough for her to do whatever she planned to at the house.

I began doing criminal record checks on her. They're called BOPs, Board of Probation checks. The BOPs came back, showing that she had a driver's license but a lot of aliases. I began to narrow them down and found out where she had used them. Soon, I saw charges of larceny and identity theft. The last town she had lived in was Centertown, Massachusetts, fairly close to Logan International Airport.

The police chief there and I had gone to police academy together. I called him and asked if he knew Shelly and her daughter.

"They're grifters," he told me. "They hook onto some guy and once they're in, they take everything the guy has."

"That's what's happening right now. The guy has two teenage daughters, and they don't know how to fight back."

"I wish we had warrants for the woman's arrest," he said, "but we don't, Jack. She leaves town too fast."

"Why didn't you guys follow up on this," I asked a little too firmly.

"Look, Jack, we're busy with other things, this wasn't a priority." he said.

Sometimes I can be a little too passionate, I thought. I thanked him and ended the conversation.

The next Monday, there I was again, in the nurse's office with the girls. They were crying and didn't want to go home. If there was any way to help them, I would have, but I knew that they would end up in the system, which meant out of their home.

"Listen," I told them, "what I'm going to show you how to do is against the law. I could get fired or worse. But I like you kids and I hate what's going on in your house."

"What are we going to do?" Rosemary asked.

"You know what a fuse box looks like?"

"Yes." She nodded. "It's in the cellar."

"You're going to go down there and pull the main switch. It looks like a lever and it bigger than the other switches inside the box," I instructed. "There's also a main fuse that is bigger than all the rest. Pull that out of the box and get rid of it. But before you do that, get some flashlights because there's not going to be any power."

"Okay."

I could tell by their intrigued looks that they were with me. Maria remained silent, taking this all in, probably thinking that this criminal stuff was a little too easy for me.

"Then you're going to go outside and walk around your house. You're going to see a box that's gray and about the size of my hand. It has a big screw in the middle of it. It should have a wire that goes from the box up into your house."

"What's that?" Sylvia asked.

"Your phone line. I want you to cut that."

They began to smile. It was as if they had gone from hopeless defeat to taking part in a spy mission.

"So there won't be any electricity and no land-line connections," Rosemary said.

"Exactly. If you don't mind not watching TV or playing on your computer, it might get the results you want. It's like driving out a rat."

"That rat could still try to go for help," Sylvia said.

I shrugged. "She can't go very far with flat tires. Do you know what a water heater looks like?" I asked.

"Is that in the cellar, it looks like a big drum?" she said with wide eyes.

"Yes, a big drum. In front of the drum, at the bottom, you'll see what looks like a little door. Pull off the front and directly inside you'll see a red knob, a dial. Turn it left to off," I instructed. "Don't worry you won't get electrocuted."

"What does that do?" Rosemary asked as she looked up from her notebook and her notes.

"It means no hot water. Shelly likes to take baths right?' I said with a smile.

They nodded in sync.

If they could do exactly what I had suggested, it might push the balance of right and wrong back in their favor. When they went to school the next morning, Shelly managed to get to a phone and called the police. They told her to come see me. You see everything that remotely deals with kids ends up with me eventually. In she came in her tight jeans, but her makeup wasn't as perfect as usual. *Kind of hard to get it right with no power in the house*, I thought. *Good girls.*

"What can I do for you, ma'am?" I asked.

"The O'Leary girls," she said. "Are you familiar with them?"

"Sure." I toyed with the file on my desk. "What's the problem with the kids?"

"I have a court order against their father, and now they're turning off the gas and the water in the house. They even let the air out of my tires."

"How do you know they're doing it?" I asked.

"Because I know, that's why. What are you going to do about these girls?"

"Did you see them do any of this stuff?" I asked.

"No" she said. But she was insistent, "What are you going to do about this?"

"Not a thing."

She was huffing and puffing and started to fidget a bit. *Good*, I thought. *She's getting angry.*

Then she glanced down at the file on my desk. It had her name written on the top in black magic marker. Spying that, she asked, "What the hell is that?"

"You might be interested in it. Take a look."

Her picture was held by a paperclip to the folder. She opened it, and the first thing that fell out was a more recent mug shot. Then her daughter's mug shot and a list of all of her aliases.

Her skin turned red, as if she'd spent a day under the hot sun. "This is a violation of my rights. Where did you get this? I'm calling my lawyer." she threatened.

"Good idea," I said, "but why don't you have a look so you won't miss any fun facts when you talk to your attorney? If I were you, I would get out of this town quickly because everything is in the works for you, lady, and time is running short. You hurt any of my kids, and you're toast," I said, motioning her to leave.

She sat there, stunned. "How could you possibly know this?"

"I know a lot of things, and you know what else I think? I bet the department of social services would love to know how you raised your daughter on the grift," I said, staring her down in an intense game of who'll blink first.

I thought of what I had told Murph. We controlled information. That was our strength. I didn't bother sharing that insight with Shelly, though. I wanted her out of my office and out of the O'Leary house. Out of our community. And I wanted the restraining order dismissed. That would happen within a week, when she failed to appear in court.

The house showed the results of her final tantrum—a trashed kitchen, pulled-out drawers, a bookcase knocked over. Nothing that couldn't be fixed. I got a hold of the father and helped him get the restraining order taken off. But if it wasn't for these little girls, things wouldn't have turned this well. When I'd see them in the halls at school after that, we'd make eye contact and high five each other—nothing elaborate just a mutual understanding of our time together. Irish twins. They had the right to remain silent, and they did. These girls had saved their family with a little bit of help from a friend.

I had helped the Irish Twins as a last resort because I knew the system would fail them. Sometimes it works, sometimes it doesn't.

CHAPTER 21

Stoners and Soup Sandwiches

In 1972, British rockers The WHO released their album *Who's Next?* It contained the classic cult song, "Teenage Wasteland." Its hook was the crescendo exclaiming, "They're all wasted!"

Certainly an anthem for my high school daze. But teenage wasteland doesn't describe this generation, my school district, or my kids. These kids do drift close to the edge when it comes to experimenting with drugs, alcohol, and other substances. And let's not forget the pull of social media and the internet. Most of my Knuckleheads could definitely benefit from digital detox.

Stoners are a reality at every school, and I don't think our problems were any worse than anyone else's. As always, I didn't want to see my students getting an arrest record for stupid behavior. That doesn't mean I went easy on the stoners. I just wanted to help them prevent ruining their lives with drugs or an arrest before they were even out of high school.

Fortunately, our alcohol problems were limited to kids with flasks, which I cheerfully liberated from their possession, and a momentary fad that a group of girls embraced—the ever-present bottle of doctored Vitamin

Water. For a short while, we were letting kids bring coffee to school, until I got suspicious, did a taste test, and realized some of those coffee drinkers were sipping spiked brew under our noses. We had been very complacent about coffee. But there is always that one percent of kids that screw it up for the rest.

We stopped coffee coming in, but kids could buy sodas around the school. That meant they could still sneak alcohol into those bottles. I contacted the soda vendors and asked if they could put a time lock on the machines.

And to Kristen, the principal, I said, "Let them only buy sodas during their regularly scheduled lunch periods."

"How's that going to help, Jack?" she asked. "They can still get drunk."

"If they are, we'll find out because they will act out in class after lunch."

The school administrators weren't all that sure. After all, part of the money from the sodas went to the school for various projects.

I decided to be blunt. "You may lose a couple of hundred dollars," I said, "but imagine the liability you're going to get hit with if a student gets drunk and falls down the stairs. It only takes one kid, one bad decision. Bad luck and trouble can be avoided, even on very small, seemingly insignificant levels."

That was the end of our unlimited soda policy and, hopefully, our alcohol problem. I knew it was only a Band-Aid response, but it was a start.

The pot smokers were a different story. They got high before school, on their lunch hours, in the parking lot, and if they were really stupid, in the restrooms.

These slow-walking chimneys are often thought to become burnouts, but I didn't find this to be the case.

They were drifting over the line, and part of my job was to keep them from staying there. These kids were throwbacks to what they imagined the sixties and seventies were all about, and they were easy to spot. Visit their homes, as I did frequently, and you'd see a picture of a big marijuana leaf on the wall. Psychedelic posters and black lights completed the décor. They were accessory nuts and couldn't help collecting the assorted bongs, papers, and pipes. Even in my little town, we had a head shop, and they frequented it.

A lot of them wore army jackets, and regardless of the weather, a stocking cap with long hair sticking out was *de rigueur* attire. They were always polite, especially to me, and they entertained no desire to cause trouble. Their only goal was to float through the rest of the day. I swear these kids wanted to be hippies or surfers. Almost all of them owned skateboards and those, combined with the stocking caps, pretty much labeled them as stoners.

"Dude," they'd greet me in the hall.

"Dude, your ass," I'd reply. "Keep moving."

These were good and intelligent kids, going through life in slow motion, but they were really harmless. However, I knew that even stoners could explode with anger, so I kept a close watch. With every good stoner conversation, they'd think they had answered some of the world's most difficult questions. When the high went away, they didn't remember what they had talked about.

I would call them all "soup sandwiches." That's a phrase used often in police departments to describe a person or a situation that is in completely fucked up. It describes something that is totally wrong and stupid, beyond stupid.

If a kid came in really reeking of pot, I would take him into my office and say, "Sit your stinkin' ass down, you soup sandwich. If I let you go to class, you'll be suspended and sent to the principal. Change into one of these."

They would take their shirts off, and I would give them a sweatshirt from my growing collection. Sometimes they would ask if they could keep the shirt. I would agree, and their clothes—after they were laundered—would become part of my personal Salvation Army.

I'd also walk them into the boy's room and have them flush their weed.

Legally, I had a lot of power over them. A kid caught driving with marijuana could lose his license until age twenty-one. Many times, I'd catch kids lighting up in a car. I'd call the kids' parents and then toy with their heads until their parents got there. I wanted their stoned brains to remember our encounter as an unpleasant experience, one they did not want to repeat.

With these particular Knuckleheads, the ones I would mercilessly mess with, I would interrogate them in a rapid-fire, Monty Python style.

These were my ganja zombies, awake but not alert, teary eyes blocking their vision, and paranoid to the point of exhaustion.

I would only allow the driver to open his window. The cloud of smoke inside set the stage perfectly. In true Boston speak and tradition, I would firmly announce to everyone, "You know you're all wicked fucked, right?" But before the pleas and apologies came, I would begin, starting with the tough questions like, "What's your name?" Then scanning the vehicle, I'd ask, "Are any of you a hostage, held against your will? Listen, you guys in the back seat, blink a few times if you want me to rescue you?" I would say, looking directly at their terror in their eyes.

I would ask for their license numbers (no one knows their driver's license number off the top of their head). To the already freaking out and paranoid driver, I would start explaining that if any answer was wrong, he was screwed and going to jail with all of his posse.

Then the questions flew. "What's your middle name? What's your favorite color? Do monkeys wear diapers? Who invented liquid soap and why? What's the terminal velocity of a seagull caught in a storm with one-hundred-mile-per-hour winds?" But I never gave them time to answer. I would, in my best hard-ass cop voice, proclaim that they were all idiots and going to jail for a very long time.

Now, unbeknownst to them because they were stoned, I had already called a parent to take custody of these real life characters right out of *Bill and Ted's Excellent Adventure.* I had them hook, line, and sinker. They were all hyperventilating, crying, or planning their escape. But I knew that because they were so high, any critical thought that might resemble a plan would be comical.

Then they became impressively repentant. "Come on, Officer Hobson," one would always plea. "Give us a break, man. You know us. We're harmless."

As soon as a parent would arrive, I would release them from their paranoid torment, search them individually, and take their herb and any other drug paraphernalia. Then, finally, I'd send them home with Mom or Dad. It was an experience I wanted them to remember for some time and, hopefully, not repeat.

I would always tell an offender, "I don't want to see this on school property so I'm going to search you every chance I get."

True to my word, if I caught these kids in the car one day and saw them in school the next day, I'd search them openly in the halls. I did that for effect. Everybody knew who the stoners were, and they had a pretty good idea why I was searching them.

I had two major concerns. I didn't want these kids driving, and I didn't want them to become burned out and useless, or more likely, cellar dwellers, that basement refuge that doubled as a bedroom and hash den.

Many times I would visit a teacher and inquire about one of my stoners. One day, the meeting was with an English teacher. I was curious about Jerry, a harmless, well-meaning kid amongst the horde who called me dude.

"How's Jerry?" I asked.

"He's slow, Jack, just not getting it."

Usually, we would have a meeting with the kid, the guidance counselor, the nurse, and myself. That's what happened with Jerry.

"You're not making it in school because you're high all the time," I said.

Sometimes, when the kid knew that we were paying attention to homework and grades, they would straighten out, pun intended. That's what happened with Jerry.

There was always a follow-up meeting to review their improvements, to make sure they didn't fall back into bad habits. Drug use would definitely sabotage their academics, but so would an arrest. I used the threat of one to get rid of the other. But, as always, an arrest would force them into a structured form of treatment or probation. Sometimes, when you treat kids like a criminal, they grew into the label. I was careful when I did that and with whom.

CHAPTER 22

The Café: 28 Minutes in Hell

S ometimes, the easiest solution to a problem was the one that was right before your eyes. That was the case with the school cafeteria. It really was a different world. But it was a predictable world if you understood the dynamics.

Even though my home base was at the high school, I was responsible for all of the schools in town. At one time, we had two elementary schools; an intermediate school for grades four, five, and six; a middle school for grades seven and eight; the high school; and the alternative high school. When they were all dealing with the same problems, such as bullying or drugs, and trying to predict where trouble would strike next, I would meet with them and frequently put on a workshop.

One of the first ways to spot trouble, I told them, was to analyze the social dynamic of the school cafeteria.

One look around my high school in the rush of the lunch period would show me a microcosm of the school. There were the stoners hanging out in their stocking caps, socking each other in the arm, and punctuating their sentences with, "Dude." I sometimes sat down with them and listened to their nonsensical conversations.

Then there were the Goth boys and girls with their pentagram notebook drawings and their doom and gloom attire. Not far from their dark world, sat a table of cheerleaders, who were easy to spot if only because of their proximity to the football team's table.

It seemed that each sport had its own table. I sometimes sat with the hockey players. As a former player myself, I could relate to these kids with the perpetual black eyes and swollen lips. Besides, it was a good place to check out the other tables.

A good distance away from the cafeteria line sat the "peanut allergy" kids, always sniffling and in eternal fear of a rouge nut. Good kids but a little too paranoid.

Then came the nerds, huddled closely together and probably talking about the robotic program they were all enrolled in. Yes, they actually built robots, some of them fighting robots that looked like vacuum cleaners from the future. Little geniuses, I used to call them, and I wasn't just stroking their egos. These kids were intelligent and had won a national competition for their designs.

The special-needs kids and kids with physical disabilities also sat together, by necessity as much as anything else. These were the kids who would hug and high-five me. I never saw them depressed.

One of the saddest was the table of loners, called wallflowers in my high school days. This was also a table with complicated personalities. Their intelligence or academic inabilities were often misunderstood, but their physical and emotional struggles with adolescence were on display out in the open for everyone to see: their acne, growth spurts, struggles with weight, glasses, and fashion. This group I scrutinized the most. I would appraise their interactions and body language and watch their eyes closely.

If they were focused on their food tray, they were usually okay. But if their eyes were wandering, searching for something or someone, perhaps that rogue bully, I became concerned. Often their very own personal tormentor who roamed unabated through the munching hordes, bullies would rock and roll and ramble for the thirty-minutes they were allotted to eat. Thirty minutes. That's an eternity for a fragile soul with a gloomy outlook on high school survival.

I would gravitate to the loner table, making eye contact with everyone, and I would sit in a conspicuous spot. That's when I became Officer Jack, a first name can be disarming with kids that were too uptight.

"Just resting my old bones," I'd tell them. "What's up? What's new and different?"

These kids were like magnets to each other. Their lack of self-esteem and torment would draw others with similar afflictions—those who suffered from the same symptoms of social awkwardness. Kids who didn't have friends would sit with other kids who didn't have friends. It was as if they found comfort hanging out with their own, but they wouldn't even make friends with each other. I guess they'd rather have no friends than be friends with those others had labeled as losers.

I found out that the kids who were getting picked on would all sit together, but when they came to the guidance counselor's office, they were alone. The dynamics of the cafeteria and the dynamics of cliques were a good way of understanding behavior, and the first step in preventing bad behavior. They were all drawn to each other. They had the same personality that led to their being picked on, the same mindset.

Seeing them as a group provided me with a snapshot of their issues. I believed that if there was going to be premeditated violence, in all probability, it was going to come from that table. Maybe not so much the shy and introverted ones, who looked glum on the outside but were regular kids on the inside, but the loner who harbored resentment and survived on hate and revenge fantasies. These kids I called my dark knights, combining the image of the mythical lance-and-shield warrior with the depression of darkness.

I knew where they were at all times, their class schedules, and where they spent their free time. They knew me because I would talk to them daily, always engaging them in conversation, telling my stupid jokes to get a sense of their moods, hoping that my intuitive powers wouldn't give me cause for suspicion.

But opposite situations evolved.

Many of my dark knights would come to me just before lunch or find their way to Maria's office. A pattern emerged, and I soon found myself with a tightly knit group, waiting out lunch in my office, safe from whatever ridicule they experienced emotionally in the cafeteria. They came almost every day from ten-thirty to twelve-thirty. As one cluster left, another would arrive. Each had an excuse or story to tell, and they trusted me, even though I had done nothing to earn their trust.

This was happening so frequently that I started taking attendance. With the approval of the principal and cooperation of teachers, I had my own land of misfit toys, and because I was the head misfit, I made the rules. I kept them active with busy work such as stapling and filing. I taught them how I liked my coffee. My loners became my friends and, because I was their friend, their status seemed to click up just enough for some to actually venture into the lunchroom. Some even became good friends with each other. "Safety and strength in numbers," I would preach to them. And I told them if they had my back, then I would have theirs. We had an understanding, a secret bond. Many times, that was all it took.

ოჲო

When some of the schools I was assigned to were having a lot of problems, I would sit down with principals, nurses, and guidance counselors.

"I want you to diagram your cafeteria," I'd tell them. And if I were met by a blank look, I would add, "Have a kid help you diagram the cafeteria. Believe me, they can show you where the nerds sit, and where the jocks are."

Those diagrams illustrated a unique social order. Just by looking at the cafeteria, they could pick out where the trouble was brewing.

More times than not, I'd get a call saying, "Jack, you were right. When we looked at the cafeteria, the kids we were worried about were all sitting together."

That's how cafeteria dynamics worked. Understanding them provided the principals with another tool to help them prevent trouble.

Because I was cheap—make that free—labor, I did numerous PowerPoint workshops on topics such as how to identify victims and how to diffuse an abusive student before the abuse escalates and the police have to intervene. I also put on workshops for the bus drivers. I knew the problems the various schools were having, so I was able to gear each presentation to a specific school. I continually stressed understanding the evidence the cafeteria provided.

"Look at who's sitting with whom, and what you'll find is that the troublemakers you haven't identified are sitting with other troublemakers you have identified," I would say. The culprits were also sitting together.

I would suspect that any middle school/high school cafeteria anywhere is like that. They all break down into a very precise social dynamic. By personality and by perception. Perception is reality to these kids. So if a kid is being called a nerd, he's going to go sit with the nerds because there is strength in numbers. They would find a comfort zone with like-minded people, knowing that they didn't have to worry about getting bullied or picked on or teased. They were all together, for lunch period at least.

CHAPTER 23

Walking the Halls

Anyone from students and teachers to school resource officers, like me, hurried, loafed, and generally moved through the school's halls like flotsam carried in streams. I pictured myself as a trawler, looking for the kids in that metaphor we've all found ourselves in at one time or another—the one about acting like a fish out of water.

I would make it a point to meet and greet every wayward traveler, the ones I'd learned to pick out by how they moved with that certain, detectable ease of being out and about when they should have been in class. It was on their faces, too, that pleasure of knowing they'd found the greatest distance from classroom to bathroom.

Police pants have nine pockets in them, and in one of those pockets, I always carried a book of passes in case a hall monitor—those assigned to snatch, grab, and berate a wanderer—began writing up a violation.

"Pete's with me," I'd say, scrawling out a permit, tearing it from my book, and handing it to the monitor. Then alone with Pete, I'd give him my *this-better-be-good* look.

"On my way to the restroom," was almost always the excuse.

"You just passed one.

"Sorry."

"Go use it," I'd say. "Then get right back to class." Before he could walk away, I'd catch him with another glance. "And wipe that look off your face before returning."

"What look?"

"The look of oblivion."

თითი

While floating along the hallways, I searched for doors held open by pens, notebooks, and other hand-fashioned doorstops. Students would perform this bit of malfeasance, sometimes stealing their way into the woods for a tryst with their latest flame, but more likely to have a butt. The excitement in the escape trumped any actual heavy petting. Teachers weren't above this trick and frequently used it to gain access to their cars, grab a quick cup of coffee, a cigarette if they smoked, or a chat with a colleague. I usually turned a blind eye to the reasons these doors were left open. But being the type of guy who pictured worst case scenarios, I'd remove the jambs and push the doors back into their locked positions, causing culprits to beg their way back through the front door, a barrier that, once it was closed, rivaled the entrance to Fort Knox.

My walks were my exercise. I wore a pedometer and compiled an average of five miles a day in my steel toed combat boots. Why steel toes? Any veteran patrolman could tell you about the first time he had his soft-toed boot run over while directing traffic or at an accident scene. I also secreted a tactical knife in my right boot.

Most police officers wore extra, hidden defensive equipment.

I'd walk up and down stairs, passing room after room, just so my presence was registered among the students. Now and then, I'd sit in on classes that interested me, like the History of American Assassinations, or the Great Civil War Battles.

One day while strolling along, I heard what sounded like uncontrolled sobbing coming from the girls' lavatory. Teachers operated within an invisible force field that kept male teachers out of the girls' room and female teachers out of the boys' room. I didn't live within those rules. I opened the door and barged in. A bunch of girls, most of whom I knew by sight, turned to glare at me.

I picked out the most familiar one. "Okay, Rhonda, what's going on?"

A voice from behind one of the stalls rang out. "None of your business. Get out."

I centered myself in front of the stall. "Who's in there?"

Rhonda came to my side. "It's Paula."

I searched the directory in my mind and found the troubled girl. "Okay, Paula, tell me what's up."

"Get out, Hobson, or I'll scream."

"Go ahead and scream," I said, "then *everyone* can rush in here."

Rhonda tapped my shoulder. "I think she's cutting herself," she said in a low voice. "She's losing it and doesn't want to live."

"Okay, Paula," I said. "I'm coming in."

"I locked the door."

"Open it, Paula, or I'll open it for you." Nothing, not a sound came from the stall. "Listen, I don't want to scare you," I said. "I'm your friend, we can figure something out." She still refused to utter a word. "Okay, I'm coming in." I raised my boot and put all my force behind it. The door popped open.

Paula was sitting on the floor, looking defeated. She hadn't cut herself, but had scratched her arms and legs with her fingernails until they were bleeding. But the scratches needed to be treated just the same. The reasons for self-inflicted injuries are personal but, in my experience, cutters perceive the pain and bleeding as cleansing, a release of hurtful memories or feelings. For some, it's as sensual as it is destructive, and it's a call for help, but on the cutter's terms.

"Get up, my friend," I said to her. "We'll take the service elevator to the nurse's office. No one will see us. Maria will know what to do and we'll keep this to ourselves."

I nodded to the other girls, until they registered their approval with signals of their own, then bent down to pick up Paula. She raised herself into my arms and wrapped her arms around my neck. "I got you," I said. "And don't worry, I'm not about to let you go."

Had I done the right thing? Sometimes I went with my gut. Anybody else handling a similar matter might have let it go the way of ambulance, hospitalization, psychiatric report.

The self-wounded girl's problem turned out to be a boy. Of course, it was always a boy. And I trusted Maria to know what to do in a case like that.

∽∾∽

Many of my hall encounters ended up going from good to bad to dangerous. Fortunately, the school's staff of experienced administrators, teachers, and counselors handled most of the problems common to such a large student body. A trip to the office could straighten out many of the troublemakers.

When I felt a student had gone way over the line and had become a danger to themselves or others, I often delayed the normal visit to the assistant principal. On occasion, I took these types of kids, suffering from psychological trauma, to their homes, making sure at least one of their parents would be there to receive us. Sitting around the kitchen table, we'd talk for hours, covering all the professional programs, in and out of school, available for disturbed teens. I'd add my knowledge as a cop, some advice based on my own experience.

I did all of this on my own time. The school was ignorant of these discussions. The kids and their parents kept them to themselves.

I judged the success of my visits by how much the kid's behavior improved. Measured against the school's normal trip-to-the-office discipline, I believed I made some headway. All of this was beyond my job description, way beyond, but I felt it proved worthy.

On most of my tours around the school, I'd run into Nick, the assistant principal, a big bear of a man. Beloved by the jocks and their parents, he'd been in the school system for forty years and had recently returned to coaching baseball, football, and basketball. Everybody trusted Nick to be there when he was needed.

He caught up with me one day as I was walking out of the gym. "Hold up, Jack."

I could tell he wasn't his usual self. "Anything wrong?"

"Lost my damn keys."

"Yeah," I said. "I do that every day."

He brushed off my attempt to appease him. "You don't understand, Jack. These are the keys to the kingdom. The master keys. The keys that will shut down fire alarms, that will override the elevator. Shit, one of the keys shuts down the whole school, the key to the room holding all the servers that run all of the computers on campus."

"What's that?" I knew all that and had a mirror set of the said keys myself, but I let him talk.

"If someone's smart enough to get in there, they can knock out the internet service for the entire school."

This was a scenario we all could relate to. I figured we'd all lost something we were told to be responsible for, something if not found in time, would jeopardize everybody who'd put their faith in us. A cop's nightmare, teachers', too, by the look on Nick's face.

"Where were you the last time you remember having them?"

"Observing Ms. Kantor's class in 232."

We went back to the classroom. He walked over to a bookshelf at the rear of the room and placed a hand on the back of a chair. "I was sitting right here," he said. "And I put my keys on top of this shelf."

I watched his hand explore the shelving in vain. "How long before you knew you might have left them there?"

He was beginning to panic. "Fifteen minutes, tops."

"Maybe Ms. Kantor has them," I suggested. "Or someone could've walked them down to the office."

He began inspecting every nook, every surface, hidden or exposed. I suspected he might be second guessing himself, so I pitched in, turning every wastebasket upside down. Finally, I felt we should move on, try to follow where he'd been before coming into this room.

Downstairs in the front office, we alerted the other administrators. It was nearing the day's final period. I picked up the intercom speaker. "This is Officer Hobson," I said, after all the connections lit up. "We are looking for a set of keys, probably twenty on the ring. They control the lights and control switches in the main computer room and the circuit- breakers for the entire school. And they open the doors needed to reset alarms and other very important things" I looked at Nick and winked. "If we don't find them," I went on, "we won't have internet power tomorrow because we won't be able to boot up the servers," hoping that little white lie might upset some students—students with the information we sought. I hoped my little lie would work, but it didn't pay off by the end of that day.

The following morning, Nick called my cell phone. "A kid just came into my office, Jack," he said. "He says he thinks he knows where the keys are."

By now, Nick was furious. He didn't think any kid would do this to him. He had always been a teddy bear. Yet, when I needed somebody to be a Pit-Bull for me, he would do that, too. That morning, his fury wasn't faked. He had been betrayed by the very people he thought revered him.

"And what did he tell you?" I asked him slowly.

"He says Mike has them."

I went through the directory in my head and found the Mike I thought was the one.

"If it's the Mike I'm thinking it is," I said, "his father's a cop." For a minute I thought Nick might have ended the call to go after this Mike kid himself. "Give me some time to handle this," I said. "I'll buzz you back soon."

Within an hour, I had Mike in my office. "Where are the keys?"

"I don't have them."

"You know what Mike, when you said you didn't have the keys your eyes looked up and to the left, as if searching for an answer, and you just told me a lie. How about I call your father, tear him away from an important case, tell him I got you down here telling me lies? Do you want him embarrassed in front of other officers who admire him?"

"No."

"Who has the fucking keys?"

"Paul does," he blurted without any thought.

"See, Mike, no hesitation with that answer and you never lost eye contact with me," I told him.

That put me back on my heels. Paul's father was a fireman, and both he and Mike's father were friends of mine.

We looked at Paul's class schedule. He was in English class and, echoing over the class intercom, I invited him to my office.

"Think hard, Paul," I said. "Where are the keys now?"

"We panicked and threw them in a pond."

"Think you can find that pond?"

"Yeah," Paul said. "I'm pretty sure we can."

"Give me a minute," I said.

"Wha—what's wrong?" Paul stammered, showing the first indication of being scared.

"Gotta call the assistant principal," I said. "Tell him I think we've found the keys to the kingdom."

"I'm really scared of Big Nick," he said.

I told him Big Nick wouldn't be mad, he'd be disappointed. I knew that was worse.

Investigations such as this one could have taken months. Because Nick and I worked so well together, we knew how to get information quickly—again, under the radar—and we had the keys back within twenty-four hours. All but Nick's personal keys, that is. They were probably still drifting in the pond. He wasn't that worried about those ones, though. His concern was that someone would break into the school, but we had resolved that threat, for one more day at least.

The kids didn't get off scot-free, though. They were suspended and given detention in a very public way. The other students needed to know that one paid a price for being a Knucklehead.

As I frequently did, I told the principal that while I was walking the halls, I would stop by the classrooms and give a little talk on character and integrity. "You have a wonderful guy in your vice principal," I told the classes I visited. "He has helped thousands of kids. I can't believe anyone could steal from him. It's like stealing from Mother Teresa."

The keys had provided a teachable moment and I didn't want to let it pass.

☙❧☙

I was enjoying a quiet walk through the halls, drinking coffee, and mentally checking off the laundry list of tasks I needed to consider, when I heard murmurings of excitement at the end of a hallway. I walked toward a gathering crowd that was huddled around a window, pointing, and talking about something outside.

"What's up, guys?" I asked.

All at once, I was bombarded by multiple opinions about what the commotion was.

Outside, on the edge of a marsh that surrounded the school like a moat, I saw a bird. A big bird, flapping its massive wings but getting no lift, no air beneath its wings to take off.

Curious, I thought.

"Officer Hobson, can't you do something?" one of the kids asked.

"What? Me?"

Upon closer observation, after I put my glasses on, I could see that the bird was a goose, a Canadian Goose, a big girl and, it appeared, frozen where it stood, tethered to the ground by an early morning flash freeze.

The previous summer, while playing golf with friends, I'd had a run-in with a Canadian Goose. So let me pause to give the golfers of the world some advice: Sparring with an angry bird to retrieve a ball that she now considers an egg is a bad idea. Trust me. Take the penalty stroke.

My young friends, whose numbers by then had grown exponentially, were practically pushing me down the stairs and out the door to save the bird. I didn't like the idea of getting up close and personal with another angry goose. They bite.

Why, I thought, *does everyone think I can solve all the problems of creatures big and small, human or not*? I was minding my own business, taking a walk and bam, flash-frozen goose rescue.

While thinking about what I would do, I stopped in the janitor's office to refill my coffee tin on my way out to the marsh. As I walked closer to the goose, it shrieked in alarm and let out a rapid fire of honks, low and loud. I was hoping that all its struggling would release it from the ice, but no luck. Then I thought coffee, hot coffee. As I made my way to the bird, I slipped, spilled my coffee, and landed on my butt. Embarrassed, with a cracked spine and ego to match, I could have sworn that the big bird was laughing at me. So was the crowd watching through the window.

But my idea had been a good one. I noticed the webbing on the goose's feet were almost free. So I refilled my mug, carefully walked as close as I could and poured the hot liquid around the big webbed feet. It shrieked louder, struggling, twisting, and protesting. Then it was free.

"Fly away now, you big pain in the ass," I yelled. But it didn't. It walked around, glaring at me as if our special time together wasn't quite over.

I backed away. It walked forward. If I walked too fast, I'd fall on my butt again.

Then, like an explosion, it launched up and over me, wings spread and honking, into the sky.

I looked at the crowd in the window, now cheering, and raised my arms in a touchdown signal. *Happy now, you little shits*? I thought with a smile as I walked back to the school with an empty coffee cup.

かかか

Occasionally, I'd wander into a classroom to visit and learn, or just to hide for a while. One class I frequented was health and hygiene, taught to tenth-grade students by my friend, Frank. The word in the halls was that he could deliver one hell of a sex discussion—the birds and the bees unplugged.

He was a great guy, a little strange but affable. He'd been a 2002 Olympic trial finalist in wrestling, a big guy with a big heart. And as a former semi-professional athlete, his speech and tone echoed the many locker rooms he'd spent much of his life in. Tough talk, right to the point, nothing sugar coated. So it was no surprise to hear his loud, plain talk while walking past his class.

"And when the guy's on top," he was saying, "the female can position herself…"

Okay, that sparked my curiosity. I stepped into the darkened room. Frank was showing a reel-to-reel black-and-white film in which a male and female writhed together in unabashed coitus on a screen he'd set up. The lens zoomed up close and personal. *Where did he get a reel-to-reel projector?* I thought. Maybe the army base— he's in the Reserves.

Never accused of being a prude, I found myself at once as intrigued and horrified as the many fifteen-year-old boys and girls in the audience. I sneaked out and waited to confront my friend.

After the class let out, I collected myself and approached him. "Frank," I said, "did you talk about this with the kids first? Letter home to parents, maybe?" I asked.

"What do you mean?"

"Like discussions on anatomy?" I was groping for words. "Male and female sex organs, the mechanics of sexual intercourse? Anything to explain the porn movie we all watched."

"Porn? You're crazy."

"Am I?" I asked. "Do you really think your students are going to tell their parents that now they understand where babies come from? No, they'll say that they watched porn. Trust me. Buckle up, my friend."

He gazed at me like I belonged in an old folk's home. "Fuck no, Jack. I wanted them to see the real deal, that way maybe they won't follow their boyfriends under the bleachers at a football game."

"You are one bat-shit-crazy dude, Frank," I said. "Good luck with that." I tried to pick my battles wisely, and I wasn't about to pick that one. "Just remember," I added, "I was never here."

❧❧❧

In any high school, when the kids were all in their assigned classes, the silence could be deafening. Often, while I was walking the floors, stairwell up and stairwell down, the lack of voices and clamor would strike me as an omen of sorts. As a police officer, I considered chaos the norm. Any threat of trouble or violence kept me busy and focused.

In this frame of mind one morning, I passed a conference room alive with the murmurings of a large group of what appeared to be coaches. Sticking my head into the room, I saw Chet, our athletic director, his usual cohorts, and many student athletes. They seemed to be quietly interacting.

"Hello," I said. "Hope I'm not breaking into anything important." Nothing came from the group, except an indescribable coldness. "Sorry," I said. "I'm going to close this door and be on my way."

I hadn't walked twenty paces down the hall when Chet stuck his head out of the room and called to me. "Jack, we need some advice," he said, as I came back to join him. "But not as a cop," he added. "As a friend."

I walked in, glancing at the others and said in a theatrical voice, "Don't suck me into any bullshit."

"We had another hazing incident," Chet said, "and we're trying to do damage control."

"Damage control?" We'd just ended the last hazing nightmare. It had turned ugly, especially for me. "Anyone here remember the last time the entire athletic program fucked up?" I didn't wait for an answer. "Okay, start from the beginning, but someone lock the door."

"A couple of days ago," Chet said, "Matt, here, a sophomore, had his head shaved by a few upper classmen." He cleared his throat. "His parents are in an uproar."

I looked at Matt and the other student athletes present. They'd all shaved their heads. "Rugby team?" I asked.

A kid I recognized as captain of this rough bunch stepped forward. "We shaved each other, for solidarity. No one was forced."

I thought of the team dynamics, how this might have happened. "Okay, why is this becoming catastrophic?" I asked.

The rugby boys began to shuffle their feet and look at one another. "You needn't answer that, boys," I told them. "But if this is going to blow up, I have to cover my ass. Does everyone understand their Miranda rights?"

Matt's voice rose from the rear of the group. "I let them shave my head. I thought it was cool. It's a team thing. I wasn't forced. It was my idea."

"How old are you?"

"I'm fifteen, Officer Hobson"

I turned to the director and coaches. "Who's having an issue with this, and has anyone from the administration even mentioned the word hazing?"

"Not yet, Jack," Chet said. "It's the boy's parents. They claim to have hired an attorney."

Awesome, I thought. *Here we go again.* As a trusted member of the school community, I did have certain unique relationships with people and organizations, our athletic program included. You might say, at times, I acted as a partner in crime to opposing groups in order to keep the career lights burning for some and stop others from becoming sacrificial lambs.

"Chet," I said. "Would it be okay if I use your private office?"

With the director's permission, I called the boy's father and asked for a meeting with him and his wife. The dad, I could tell, was very defensive and mentioned the word *attorney* many times. But he finally agreed to a meeting.

"At the school?" he asked.

"At the police station." I let him think about that a minute. "You've been very vocal," I said. "Have you contacted the school?"

"No, I haven't."

"Fine," I said. "Can we keep it that way until we get together?"

"Yes, I think we can do that."

We agreed on a time and I hung up. Then I sat in the director's chair for a moment, hoping the dad wouldn't show up with a lawyer.

The clandestine meeting was held in the community room of the police department, a space in the back of the station where there was no hint of official police interrogation. Matt, the boy in question, brought a teammate for support. His parents, of course, were present, along with the athletic director and me.

The father started his diatribe immediately, threatening everything from civil action to an apocalyptic maelstrom against the school. He looked directly at me. "I'll have your job, your badge," he said. "We intend to go to the media about this."

I listened, struggling with my patience. "Okay, I get it. You're upset." I turned quickly to his wife. "Mom, what's your take on this?"

The woman looked at her husband, dropped her head, and remained silent.

"Oh—kaay," I said, drawing out the two syllables. "Before I read you your rights, I want you to change your tone and listen very carefully to me. If a crime was committed, I will pursue it professionally with methodical temperance. So, understand that."

Everybody, including Chet, looked like I'd pulled a gun out of my holster. "You have the right to remain…"

The father had found his voice. "Wait a fucking minute," he said. "You're advising *me* of *my* rights?"

I regarded him calmly. "Yes," I said. "Did you not just threaten my job? The job of the athletic director? Did you not threaten to bring havoc upon the school?"

He glanced at his wife. She stared at me. Matt stared at his buddy. The athletic director closed his eyes.

"Bullshit," the father finally shouted.

I let that ring in the air for a second or two. "Do you have an attorney?"

"You're damned right I've got an attorney."

"Do you want him here, or shall we schedule another meeting with him present?"

If looks could kill, I'd be lying on the floor, breathing my last breath. I'd called his bluff. The attorney's hourly rate to be in the room with us, along with all the negative exposure his kid and teammates would suffer, stopped the father from making good on his threat.

"Enough is enough," the mother shouted. "We're not doing this. We're not going to destroy our son's chances for a normal high school experience." She shook her fist at her husband. "Matt told you it was his idea to have his head shaved."

"But we didn't give permission," the father said.

"Dad, you never give permission for anything," Matt said, his eyes shining with tears. "And you've never even been to a rugby game."

I'd just won a big pot in this game of wills, but I decided to go for the jugular. "Now, I understand hazing is a hot-button, an emotional issue," I told him, trying to lure the father into another hand. "You're going for publicity and a civil suit. This is about money, isn't it?"

Silence. Dead silence.

I, again, turned to the mother. "Do either you or your husband intend to contact the school or the newspapers?"

"No," she said.

It was time to get down to business. "A threat to commit a crime is in itself a crime," I said, enunciating every word in a slow, even manner. "Destroying careers, slandering a school, and accusing others of assault, kidnapping, and maiming are offenses punishable by powers greater than me. Trust me. Such actions never end well."

"So, where do we go from here?" the athletic director asked the father.

He folded, not an apologetic type of fold, but close enough. The mother seemed relieved. The boy was happy, but visibly stressed. He would remain on the team.

Happy ending?

No telling, I thought. I asked everyone to leave but the father. Then I motioned to a chair and he sat. I dropped into a seat across the small desk from him and gave him a minute to get it together.

Finally, he raised his eyes and I saw an opening. "This could have been a runaway train," I told him. "One that could kill an already wounded program, a program designed for kids like your son."

"All that legal stuff you were spouting—"

"Legally, I was in bounds," I said. "You don't want to test me on that."

"I guess I understand."

I extended my hand across the table. He shook it. "You ought to go see Matt play a game," I said. "Lots of people have been telling me he's a damn good player."

"Yeah?"

"Tough sport, rugby."

"Yeah?"

"Maybe the toughest sport out there." I lifted myself out of my chair, sighed like an old veteran. "You think maybe that's why they shaved their heads? You know, to kind of set themselves apart from other kids who can't find the determination, the resolve?"

I didn't know if I'd replaced that look of winning a lawsuit in his eyes with what he might see in a son who wanted his father to watch him play rugby. But I got him to the table.

ᘓᕉᘓᕉ

Afterthoughts:

The original "Don't ask, don't tell" activity:

Hazing. It's against the law. I don't condone it. I have arrested students and adults for their participation. I have investigated hazing and I have interviewed and observed the accused and lamented with the victims—and there is always more than one—within the context of the school and, by extension, team sports.

It is no longer an adolescence prank, a condition of team membership, or a ticket to the game.

And I'm not going to gain any points here, but "kids" do not discover hazing on their own. There is no magical osmosis zapped into their head.

Somewhere there is an adult or older person, an ex-athlete in a supporting role, in tandem with the history or legacy of that particular sport.

Let me draw a line in the sand. All too often hazing is reported as a sexual assault, a perversion of power, control, and humiliation.

Crossing that line gets the suspect or suspects—and hazing often requires the complicity of more than one knucklehead—a trip to the courthouse.

Only a certifiable delinquent, or those contributing to the delinquency of a minor, with bad intentions, would haze alone, and in that context, hazing becomes a major crime, a capital offense. A throw-away-the-key offense in my mind.

I recognize hazing for what it is, and I understand it from a law enforcement and personal perspective. And, yes, I have been hazed.

I have pondered the reasons, motivation, and misguided requisite idea of hazing, for trust and the cohesiveness of a team—misguided meaning that a potential team member might flinch, chicken-out, have a low threshold for pain, pick your excuse. It's all fruits of that poison tree.

And, as the weak link does, it breaks. And talks and tells and brings into the light what should remain covered in shadow.

I played hockey as a kid in the 1970s. Being hazed or initiated—and, by virtue thereof, accepted as a team member—was not only accepted, but anticipated. It meant something and it was in no way labeled as criminal. It was a tangible action with hopeful results. It was a rite of passage then, back in the day.

Let's make a quick distinction between bullying and hazing. Synonyms, right? Not really. Bullies do not want their victim to be part of a group, any group, since their goal is to humiliate, degrade, and shame their targets. It doesn't work so well if the odds are even.

Hazing is different because it involves a group dynamic and coercion. Coercion, intimidation, and duress are subtle-but-evil-and-powerful step-brothers.

And don't ever underestimate the "team effect," that is, the power welded by a team's aura when a young boy, who, by himself and on his own, may be weak, passive, and impressionable, but as a team member he becomes part of something big, so big it radiates confidence and a sense of attachment—attachment for some only second to that of a mother.

But we know that it survives today in school locker rooms, in secret chambers behind secret walls, and at sleep over's and summer training camps, and anywhere else where a good beating separates the boys from the men.

Hazing, it's not cool. Not cool at all.

CHAPTER 24

Room 139

My daily walk-a-bouts were never complete until I visited the realm of the superheroes. They preferred to be called superstars, but superheroes seemed, in my mind, more appropriate. This was the special-needs class. Room 139. It was inhabited with the happiest, most-loving, and generous souls this side of heaven.

I almost always brought gifts. They delighted in plastic police badges, pencils, key chains, and stickers that always ended up on my forehead before I left.

The size of these students' hearts—their incorruptible innocence—was the great equalizer. The law allowed many of them to stay in school until age twenty-one. After that, it was either a group home or stay at home with their parents. Some were able to get jobs. In high school, however, anything was possible for them. Clarice, for instance, didn't let Downs Syndrome rob her of finding joy in everyday life.

She was part of the group who elected me the chief taster when the class embarked on cooking lessons, sending the smell of cookies, brownies, and cake wafting through the halls. Each Tuesday, the class created a menu and put one in everyone's mailbox. They advertised freshly made fare for about two dollars. Class members were the cooks and servers, and they personally delivered each meal to its proper recipient. Café 139 was a huge success, and the pride of accomplishment made everyone feel good.

One day as I was walking by, I heard music—*The Twist*, by the Chub Man himself, Chubby Checker—playing loudly. The laughter inside Room 139 was voluminous and electric. So I went inside, and without warning, I was twisting with my friends in a tight circle, feeling like a ball being sucked into a whirlpool. I was hooked. Clarice jumped up beside me in a blue-and-yellow ballerina hippo costume. We danced, and the screams and happy chants got louder, primal, and innocently wonderful. At some point, I remember silly string being sprayed haphazardly around in a storm of pink and yellow florescent glitter and confetti. It was Mardi Gras and the Saint Patrick's Day parade in Dublin all rolled into one.

Some had fashioned capes from scrap fabric. Some had on thick snow gloves. Others wore swimming goggles, the round ones that make your eyes look like fish eyes. Someone tucked a towel into the back of my collar, and I strutted in my very own Batman cape.

My academic sensibilities knew that laughter, play, and a sense of freedom, inclusion, and safety were so very important to the progressing needs of these special students. That, and it was just plain fun, a welcomed way to recharge my batteries.

Then, like an angry babysitter, our principal, Kristen, came storming in, shut off the music, and scolded no one in particular. "This is a school," she shouted. "What are you? Animals?"

A few of my cohorts pointed instinctively at me. Oh, sure, blame the cop.

I didn't answer because I was hiding behind Clarice, and I left as quietly as possible. The strange looks I was getting in the hall puzzled me, until I remembered the silly string.

Then over the police radio, my dispatcher was telling me to respond to a car accident, an MVA. The only information was that a pickup truck, traveling at a high speed, had jumped the sidewalk in front of the high school, sped about one-quarter mile across a farmer's field, and collided with a stone wall. One occupant, air bags deployed.

I ran to my cruiser, called for other officers and EMS, and drove across the very damp field to where the vehicle's point of impact put the truck up onto a stone wall about six feet off the ground. They was no smoke or fire, nothing leaking as far as I could tell, so I climbed into the cab, turned off the ignition and checked on the driver. He was a student, about seventeen, and unconscious. His breathing was labored. Thanks to his airbag, he only had a cut on the bridge of his nose. All indications suggested a seizure, so I kept his airway open and rubbed his chest with my knuckles to try to stimulate a response.

He started to come around.

By that time, the firemen had arrived and had taken over the scene, readying the driver for transport. My firemen friends gave me their best *are-you-shitting me* look. I just shrugged. A crowd gathered around us. I stayed until the boy's mother arrived and accompanied him in the ambulance to the hospital.

The kid in the accident was one of the lucky ones. No serious injuries.

A few days later, his mother put an ad in the local paper, praising the fire department and the quick response of the police. And she wanted to shout out a special thank-you to the police officer who was first on the scene to help calm her boy. So at the bottom of the article was a heartfelt thank-you to the cop with the silly string and cape covered with pink and yellow glitter.

I refused to confirm or deny the pink and yellow glitter.

From then on, whenever I encountered Clarice in the hall or the cafeteria, she jumped up and launched into the Twist. I joined her.

CHAPTER 25

Ain't Gonna Be No Rematch

Jerry, a football player, started a fight with a smaller, relatively unknown kid, determined to show him who was boss. He got the surprise of his life when the kid knocked him on his arse—flat out like a lizard drinking.

We separated the kids, pushed the giant-killer aside, picked up Jerry and his pride, and called their parents. When Jerry's father showed up, I sensed there could be some anger. He seemed pissed off but I wasn't sure where his anger was centered.

As was the procedure, we had put the kids in different rooms.

Jerry's father looked through the glass into the room next to ours. "Who's that?"

"That's the other part of this fight," I said.

"No way." He grew even more outraged, clearly not believing that his big strong son was beaten by that skinny little kid.

"If they fight again, the results will be different," he said.

"Are you telling us that you want a rematch?" I asked him.

"The results would be different, I guarantee you."

"You're out of your mind," I told him.

We soon had a confrontation between the dad and the assistant principal, who was handing out the suspension. Imagine what the pressure on this kid at home was. His father missed the whole point—that fights in school are simply not allowed. He wasn't interested in those consequences. He was interested in how the fight ended up.

Finally, he was getting in our face so much that he was really close to being disorderly, not to mention getting handcuffed. He was yelling, his neck bulging. "I can't believe you let this happen to you," he shouted at his son.

Jerry was crushed. Not only did he have a black eye, but he was getting an emotional black eye from his father because he hadn't lived up to expectations.

"You don't seem to realize that if we wanted to, this kid wouldn't be playing sports anymore because of his behavior," I told him. "Either you deal this in an appropriate way, or that's the end of football. Sports are a privilege."

The father was as big a problem as his son. In fact, as was often the case, the father was the real problem.

Consistent parenting means not giving the kids too long a leash. It means always being there for the kids. Parents need to take the time, maybe before they go to bed, to talk one-on-one with their children about their day. The kids must feel that they are part of something important in the family.

As I dealt with the kids, I could see how their behavior coincided with the type of parenting they were getting or, in too many cases, not getting. Overall, parenting styles fall into three basic groups: Authoritarian, Permissive, and Neglectful.

Authoritarian parents have high expectations for their children, and they express those expectations in two ways, induction and coercion. Induction means involving the child in conversation, discussing values and behavior, and in short, listening. Kids from this environment tend to do well in school, and they appear well-adjusted.

Contrast them with kids from a coercive environment. These my-way-or-the-highway parents rule by fear, threats, and the removal of privileges. It's no surprise that their kids are the ones who act out, are unhappy and withdrawn. Their school problems center on peer relationships, which are often marked by hostility and aggression. Overall, these kids lack parental support and interaction. No one is listening to them, which often results in problems in school and poor academic skills.

Indulgent parents want what is best for their children, but all too often they aren't able to provide direction or expectations. The kids often drift because it's left up to them to decide what rules to follow. Indulgent parenting is ironic in that despite the parents' involvement with their kids and, despite their nurturing, they are absent from an important part of parenting. As a result, they don't provide guidelines. The kids from these homes can be more impulsive and less mature when compared to children from the other parenting styles. They tend to be self-centered, impulsive, disobedient, and rebellious.

Neglectful parenting is detached and uninvolved. It lacks the warmth of the indulgent parenting and the control of authoritarian. No limits are set because no one seems to care. Neglectful parenting can also mean dismissing the children's emotions and opinions. Parents are emotionally unsupportive of their children, but will still provide their basic needs, such as food and housing. Neglectful parenting can stem from a variety of reasons. They include the parents prioritizing themselves, lack of encouragement on the parents' parts, financial stresses, lack of support, and addiction to harmful substances. In adolescence, these kids may show patterns of truancy and delinquency.

Parents need to wake up. Children learn from their environment. Whatever communication, good or bad, the parents are having, the kids soak up like a sponge. The black slates of childhood filled with all kinds of bad ideas and etiquette. A lot of times, they are acting out and the parents don't know why. Kids are unseen victims. We're all affected by nature and nurture.

When I used to break up fights, I would ask a kid, "What's going on?"

When he tried to explain that the other kid bumped into him or called him a name, I would say, "No, what's going on at home?"

"There are no perfect families," I would tell them. "What's going on with your family is their business, but does it really make you feel better getting in a fight or swearing at a teacher?"

These kids were releasing emotions they picked up at home. While schools deal with such behavior by suspension, that isn't going to solve the emotions that caused it. Almost always it was trouble in the family or the extended family.

Parents expect educators to be surrogate parents the eight hours that their kids are in school. When you're dealing with the population of a small town in one building, you can't be the parents. At the school, we had all of the resources, the skill sets, but we only got the chance to use them when the kids acted out. The parents were the ones in a position to detect a problem before it escalated.

A lot of kids learned through their mistakes, or outgrew bad behavior as if they just got too old to act that way.

"Once you survive high school, your life is going to change in a very good way if you let it," I'd tell them. "Just survive high school."

Jerry, the football player, survived school in spite of his father.

The father was so upset that day, we had to get the other kid out of the room. I didn't want him to start another fight. After the dad screamed for an hour, they left, but not before I told him, "If anything happens to this other kid, if he has so much as a scratch, even outside of school, you know where I'm going first. And that, my friend, is both a threat and a promise," I said with an intense conviction.

This was just a small piece of Jerry's life, and I couldn't help wondering what the rest of it was like. He was used to fighting. It was a way of life for him.

"How do you think Dad is treating Jerry at home?" I asked the assistant principal.

"I can guess, Jack."

The fighting and the violence seemed to be a by-product of the way Jerry was treated. Seldom did parents come in looking for help for their kids. They would rather deal with the provocation. The why, the who, and what happened. Ultimately, they wanted to blame the other kid, the other kid's parents. Or us.

CHAPTER 26

*The Web: Partying, Bullying, Sex,
and Digital Detox*

Out of roughly nineteen hundred kids in the school, about three quarters of them were online, or about 1440 students—online meaning able to access the internet at school or home. Because I was missing so much, I had no choice but to join them. More than a few parents began bringing in Facebook pages, as well as, print-outs of other easily accessible webhosts and sites.

These pages depicted their kids' opinions, ideas, and plans, and other information they offered willingly and unabashed, believing that their parents had no way of finding out about their friendships and secrets. Worried parents uncovered pictures of their children at house parties and at other undisclosed venues. They saw underage drinking, smoking, and sexual touching between their kids and kids that they had never met.

I knew that these kids were riding the wave of social media to advance their enchantment with a boyfriend or girlfriend, mildly addicted to their ideas of what love is and the apocalyptic effect of jealously and unrequited affection. Plus, the internet gave them a sense of freedom and an invincibility so common in teenagers. This shocked their parents, but confused them even more.

I was adamant in my belief that this was a parental problem and that serious supervision and rules about internet access lay with the adults at home, not the SRO at the high school. But when presented with something tangible that I could investigate, I realized I had to dig a little deeper to find out if the internet gossip was real, or if the kids were just posturing.

I decided to set up two dummy Facebook accounts. That wasn't new or unique to police work, but it was new and unique to me because I was a newbie when it came to investigating any kind of cybercrime. I posed as both a fourteen-year-old boy and a fourteen-year-old girl who lived in the town. The thing about social media is that you don't need any particular skills to jump into the pool, which makes it too user-friendly and dangerous. I quickly understood that naïveté and reckless abandon online breeds identity theft, bullying, and threats that gobble up self-esteem and overwhelm young targets—hence parent involvement, which seemed to always lead to me.

I knew enough about the demographic of Facebook-like sites I could remain innocuous. I blended in. My purpose was to get myself friended by the people I wanted to investigate. When kids were arranging fights or when girls were threatening other girls because they looked at their boyfriends, I couldn't investigate on my own without questioning a lot of kids. On Facebook, I could just go in and monitor the page of him or her in question. I didn't have to talk to anyone.

I used that phony identity to investigate events that were already in progress. I wasn't fishing for information. Some parents were angry and disgusted in defense of their children's use of the internet, but if cornered, I would prove to these dissenters just how easy it was to obtain information, especially on Facebook. It was easy to bait young people, sometimes it was as easy as sending a request for information using a forged link. If asked for information, you could look at the requesting incoming link by rolling your mouse over the link and seeing if it matches what was in the e-mail. If you saw "https" the website or email was much more secure than if "https" was not present. The "s" in "https" means secure. If an e-mail contained words like emergency or urgent or put a time limit on the request for personal information, it was most likely a phishing expedition.

And if an e-mail was sent from Facebook, attached to your account, and asked for updated information as generic as a date of birth, age, zip code, or telephone number, beware. Legitimate companies don't function that way. I obtained a plethora of demographic information from selected students to show their parents how naïve and at-risk their children were. But the issues I was fishing for were specific and I wouldn't go into anybody's account without an investigative reason. It would do me no good. If they were arranging a fight or a party with other kids, I knew where my usual suspects were.

I would comment just enough so that they knew that I—this fake kid—was in the forum. If I targeted a kid, and there was a conversation that was suspicious, I could get to them before they did anything. Then I could bring their parents in. I would call them and have a meeting at the school.

Usually it went pretty well and resulted with what I was hoping for—parental involvement. As we sat in my office at school, I would print out what I had, give it to the parents, and get them on Facebook so they could see what I was seeing.

My hope was that they could monitor their kids. Some were shocked completely because they weren't involved enough to know what their kids were doing online. I would help them pick out software to monitor their children's websites. My choice was to have them block those sites, but most kids knew how to get around that.

I never told kids or parents that I had a fake identity. The kids were always shocked that I had gotten the information.

"Look," I would tell them. "You have friended or befriended over two hundred people, any one of them could have turned on you. I have information from a lot of people who've been on your page." That was how I got around the issue of how I knew what I did. The reality was that police controlled information, that's what we do.

On Thursday or Friday, I would go online and find out where the weekend parties were. I would just pick a kid I knew was in the mix of everything. I'd jump in at some point and ask, "What's up for the weekend? Where's everybody going?"

Everyone would respond with, "Tom's house," or "Out in the woods," or maybe, "The beer is stashed in my backyard by the fence."

These messages might be true, or they might be wishful thinking. Only one way to find out. Once in school, I would meet up with the kids I knew hung with the crowd I was watching online and have a conversation with them. Then I would ask them about the weekend. If I could pinpoint a house where something large was being planned, I would notify the parent in charge.

"Are you going to be gone Friday night?" I would ask, knowing the answer. "If so, you might be interested in this post someone gave us from Facebook. Their plans include alcohol, marijuana, and boys and girls together, left to their own devices."

The parents were often surprised, but it wasn't a contest of he-said, she-said. I had the printed proof of what their kids were up to. That was my biggest goal—to let parents parent their own kids, even when the behavior was almost criminal. I didn't want to have to send a kid into the juvenile court system and then back to his parents. I tried to eliminate the whole court piece. That's what the court's preference is anyway. Bringing the parents into the loop was always my end game.

Parties weren't the only activities that Facebook helped me deter. Bullying was a swift, cruel sport that traveled much faster through cyberspace. Kids who wouldn't threaten someone else in the halls, turned into online devils. They would bombard girls with threats and exclude them from activities. Then the activity would leave Facebook and slowly enter one-on-one activity in the halls, where it very well might explode into a fight. The internet was just a vehicle to bring a verbal threat face-to-face with the victim. Threats would build that eventually led to a confrontation or a yelling match.

Depending on how many were bullying the other kid, they would ultimately break him or her. It's easier to gang up on the internet. It was just a keystroke, and they were aligned with the bullying group.

If I would see a fight and not know what it was about, I would have to work backward to do the investigation, but by then, they'd moved onto to other similar situations. Every time we had incidents that resulted in an arrest, I'd get in touch with the principal.

"Let's round up the senior class and get them to auditorium," I'd tell her, knowing that we needed to stop what was happening that day and not next week. Other schools would have a bullying situation where someone was badly hurt, but it would take them two or three weeks to find a speaker to handle it. I wasn't going to wait two weeks.

If I wanted to talk to the whole school, they would do a series of assemblies. Sometimes, right before one of these, I'd make a public arrest and handcuff the kid in the hallway. I did that on purpose to show everybody what could happen.

Once I had the kids assembled there, I'd ask the teachers to leave. Then I would do my best to connect with the kids. I would talk about the new crimes that were becoming enforceable on the internet. I saw this type of crime as continuing, so I wasn't just dealing with prevention as was done in many workshops. I was trying to stop it, and I used brutal honesty. I'd get down off the stage right down with them. I would get down and dirty with the kids.

"This is what you're going to lose," I'd tell them, "starting with respect." Then I would go onto to losing a job, losing an education. I would use the worst case scenario for these kids and make it clear I wasn't scolding them. I was there to try to right a sinking ship. I wouldn't threaten them. I would just tell them the truth. These assemblies had the same social construct as the cafeteria. I knew who I was talking to and where they were sitting.

What made some of these assemblies so effective was my interaction with the kids. Some would argue that their behavior wasn't criminal, and I would tell them the truth about that. Some assemblies took a half-hour. Others were ninety minutes or longer. If they were interacting, I would not shut that off.

Did they help? I think, in many cases, they did. When parents came in worried about some discovery they had made about their kids' online lives, I could say, "We are addressing this. We know about it, and here is what we've done."

If we had a problem and I needed to have an assembly, I would text the parent list with a low-priority but high attention message. I never sent high-priority messages, knowing we would have the parking lot full of parents coming to get their kids. These were FYI messages.

I would tell them that because of a recent incident, we held an assembly that addressed bullying, cyber bulling, and threats. A lot of parents were thankful we notified them, but a lot were uneducated about what we were talking about. My goal was to get them interested in what was happening, to ask questions, and to listen.

The internet wasn't our only electronic challenge. Along with the popularity of the cell phone, and a litany of tech-savvy hand-held devices, came what I called the Mirror Image Cases. They went something like this: a girl, fifteen-years-old, takes a picture of herself in the mirror of the girls' restroom. The boy responds with a picture of himself. If these photos could be kept private, between just them, then this freaky affair probably would have taken its course. By the way, the young models in these private photo shoots were often sans clothes, *nomaspantalones*, or in varying stages of undress.

Instead, they would send a photo to two people who sent it to two other people, an out-of-control, exponential nightmare. Even though the kids could obscure their faces, I could always narrow the identity search down to a phone number. If a boy or girl were having a shoving contest in the hall, I would break it up and pick up the cellphone and, with a little searching, we would know the reason for the fight as soon as we looked at the screen. No secrets in a high school hallway, power and popularity too desirable to withhold information.

I would preach to the students, "If you put yourself out there, it's all in the game, fair play is not considered, all is fair in love and text messages. Attach a picture, and you are the one who stepped on the angry snake. The internet is an unforgiving place."

They saw this as personal between them, a sacred bond, a deviance shared. When they lost control and couldn't contain it, that's when the emotions exploded. That became very agitated and touchy because the law is very clear. It cannot yet tell the difference between a kid and a predator.

The law sees facts not intentions. There is no artificial intelligence working in tandem with our brain. No safety network or interpretation referee. I would try to make the sharing of confidential information appear as an internet threat.

I had to lecture kids about how threatening and embarrassing it was, had to get them to realize it was wrong on so many levels. And it was illegal.

Furthermore, I had to make them understand how many people were affected by a text or picture or inappropriate sexual comment. I would mention their grandparents, their cousins, and their extended family— those not literally on the home front, but those who would be bothered, embarrassed, and disappointed.

They would become defensive, raise their forced fields and ask, "What does my grandfather have to do with this?"

And I would say, "Exactly."

CHAPTER 27

A Walk Outside the Walls

I've saved this story as one of the last because it represents everything I loved about my job and those kids. It's about an outcast, of course, a kid who was drifting. His name was Tony. He was a clean-cut, fifteen-year-old who came into the school as a sophomore. His parents had decided to utilize our school district's choice policy of accepting students from other areas, as long as they paid a tuition fee.

Although we were a public school, a student from another district, even another town, could choose us over his or her previous school. Often, parents believed we were better equipped, or simply more convenient, than other jurisdictions to handle their kids.

One of the guidance counselors called me over one day, early in the fall semester. "Jack, we're trying to figure out why Tony isn't doing very well lately."

I brought a picture of the boy up in my mind. A well-groomed kid, he hadn't been much of a problem. "Transfer student, school choice kid," I said, still trying to define him. "He's never been able to fit in much, has he?"

"He proved he can be a fairly good student at his last school," the counselor said, "but he hasn't settled in yet."

"In what way?"

"He has pretty much quit doing any homework. Won't engage with anyone, let alone his teachers. Started sitting alone, sniping and snapping at other students."

Sniping and snapping, I thought. I have an older sister who called me a snipe, still does sometimes—once a big sister, always a big sister.

I'd learned that new students usually followed two paths. They chose to expand their personalities and quickly took the opportunity to latch onto some new friends, or they turned silent in an effort to distance themselves from anything having to do with school.

For the next day or two, I did my best to find out more about this boy, who evidently felt he no longer fit in. I'd dealt with kids like Tony many times before. Maybe I'd find something to go by if I examined my own life's choices when I was young and in his shoes. With each stage of my life, from grade school to graduate school, from good jobs to better jobs to a career and professional obligations, I had toiled and struggled a bit to fit in. It took a while, but change doesn't get easier with age.

Thinking this, I managed to catch up with him alone in the hall before the end of the week. "Hey, Tony," I said, fronting him so he wouldn't bolt. "What's been going on?"

"Not much," he said, eying me as though measuring my stocky frame, which wasn't much taller than his, most likely spying a look at my uniform and all the gadgets on my gun-belt.

"Sometimes, transferring to a new school can be tough." What I meant was, how lonely one could feel, but

I stayed clear of any words that might imply he was weak.

He hesitated then gave me a defeated look. "I just don't like it here," he said. "I don't like the classes. I don't like the teachers."

I tried to let my eyes tell him that I'd heard this before from hundreds of kids. "Give it some time," I said. "You didn't have any problems at your old school." Hearing about his accomplishments from his previous school didn't seem to encourage him. I felt right then that he was pushing back at me, that he needed space. "Do me a favor?"

He showed little enthusiasm. "What?"

"Do the best you can to work with the guidance counselor," I told him. "You need to at least show some effort. I know it's not easy to talk to adults about problems but my job here is to be a resource. Don't be afraid to talk to me. Anything we talk about stays between us. I'm a good listener. You know where my office is, right?"

He nodded.

About a week later, I heard that Tony had skipped a couple of days. The following week, he was also absent a lot. I checked to see if his parents had been dropping him off each morning. They had, driving him to school every day, but he just hadn't gone in to his first period class.

The assistant principal in charge of discipline was at her wit's end with him. She gave it a day or two more then called his parents and arranged a meeting. I was invited.

After a few words with Tony and his parents, I suggested to the principal that she leave things to me, at least for the time being.

Everyone eye-balled me, like the next move was mine. I patted Tony's shoulder. "Let's you and me take a walk."

"Am I in trouble?"

I thought about his question. Was he? "Other than deciding you're evidently going to quit school and worry your parents and teachers to death," I said, "you're probably not in any big trouble, not with me, anyway…yet," I said with a smile.

A few minutes later, he slowed down and gave me a look. We were behind the school, closing in on a small stand of trees. When we'd reached the edge of a wooded area, he seemed a bit wary about where this path would end.

I'd grown up in woods not far from there and was comfortable in the surroundings. When I was a kid, my friends and I would spend our days in the woods, playing in the ponds, walking barefoot in the little rivers. We would walk barefoot in little streams at a local golf course feeling for golf balls, and we would sell them back to golfers. No overhead—it was a good deal. That was better than any video game. We played. We learned. About team work, competition, free enterprise, and being part of something: a crew, a group, a gang of good kids.

Soon, Tony and I came upon a pond. The afternoon sunlight was dimmed by a thin fog that had rolled in. I directed his gaze to a big rock at the water's edge. "Hear that low guttural sound, like a croak?"

"Yeah," he said. "What is it?"

"That's a Spring-Pepper Bullfrog. By the sound of it, she's a girl. It's mating season for a lot of air-breathing reptiles and other water creatures, so stay sharp. Just like human mothers, these wild things are very protective of their nests and everything in them. These particular frogs can lay more than a thousand eggs, and when they hatch, they become pollywogs. They look like minnows, little fish, until they start to grow legs and webs on their feet and, almost overnight, they're full-fledged frogs. Cool, right?"

He seemed mildly interested. "Yeah."

"But there are a lot of things, hungry things, in this pond that might eat the tadpoles. A snake or a bigger frog, or even a bird. Some birds feed off of the insects that float on the water. Sometimes, the tadpoles swim up toward the sun and, zap, they're toast. See that?" I said, just loud enough to get his attention.

He stopped. "Holy shit, what is it?"

"A snapping turtle," I said.

"He sure is big."

"Yah, but I've seen much bigger, uglier, and meaner ones in this pond so watch your step. They hide in the mud. And it's not a he. She. Big, bad Mama. Look at the head on her," I said, balling up my hand. "It's big as my fist." I opened my hand and showed him a scar on my index finger. "They bite and they hurt. Battle scar from a snapper when I was about your age," I told him. I began to lead him on a trip around the pond. "Especially the females. At this time of the year, it's baby time in the wild and in the water, so you'll notice more females. Watch that one. I want to show you something. Ever seen a turtle's nest?"

"A nest? No, never," he whispered, not wanting to upset Big Mama.

As we strolled, I pointed out other turtles. "There's a white spotted turtle. They don't bite, but they're hard to catch because they're fast."

"What if I stuck my finger in its mouth, would it bite then?" he asked.

"If someone stuck a finger in your mouth, would you bite?"

"You bet I would."

"There's you answer, Einstein."

He laughed.

I walked him farther in—about ten more feet—put on my gloves, knelt down, and started to dig softly, removing the wet leaves and moss and mud that had been perfectly placed for cover and protection. Soon, I was soaked up to my knees. Not far away, the mama turtle moved off a rock.

I looked up at my partner. "Are you watching that turtle? I hope so, because she's watching us. When it's dark, she'll crawl over and sit on the nest, keeping it warm and protecting it from the fisher cats or bog cats and other rodents that hunt at night."

"What's a bog cat?"

"They're bigger than a house cat, very solid-looking with natty hair and very sharp claws. And they're fast. When they meow, it sounds like a roar, a roar from a much larger animal. They're nasty and they attack. Most animals run away from people. These wild cats attack. They live in the cranberry bogs," I told him. "I'll have to show you a picture of one. You don't see too many during the day unless they're sick. You still watching the mama turtle?"

"Yeah, I'm keeping track of her." He actually sounded a bit excited.

"Air breathers don't bury their eggs in the water," I said. "Here, look at these turtle nests I'm turning up." The eggs were visible. I pointed them out to Tony. "Like chicken eggs," I said.

"Only bigger."

"And softer. More like prunes," I said. "They lay about fifteen." I watched him. His face had taken on a glow from the afternoon haze. "Did you know that in a part of India, there is a Hindu group that believes one of their goddesses was reincarnated as a particular type of turtle, and that type of turtle is worshiped?"

"Really?"

"Yeah." I grinned. "Look it up on the internet. Search the god turtles of India," I told him.

I could tell he was enjoying himself. I had gone through adventure training as a DARE officer and over the years, I'd introduced many kids to natural environments like this one. Tony, I was sure, hadn't heard the lore of this area. "You know," I said to him, "this is a two-thousand-year-old Native American burial ground. Superstitious folk, those natives. Did you know that Indian Spirits never, ever die?"

"Really?"

"Lots of paranormal activity has been reported around here, going back to what might be the very first-documented UFO sighting in 1799, found in a journal that belonged to a college professor. A whole lot of strange entries in that book."

He looked up into the tree limbs above him then back at me, a slight smile on his pale face. "You believe that stuff?"

"Why not? There's got to be a billion stars out there and a whole lot of planets. Why would we be the only planet with life?" I said. "One of the latest reports was from a police officer, not that long ago. Said he saw a triangular craft of some type with red and white lights, flying upside down, and then it seemed to crash head-first into the ground, but there was no wreckage and no impact craters. We also tested for gamma and radioactive gases. Nothing."

Then I told him the difference between the words terrestrial and extraterrestrial.

He looked at me and I could tell he was trying to process something. "I get it," he said, smiling. "ET was an extraterrestrial. I get it."

Were we connecting? I wasn't sure. I thought of going into the many reports of a Bigfoot-type monster emerging from the legendary Hockomock Swamp nearby, but didn't want to press my luck. Instead, I pointed at his feet. "I'll tell you a real cop story that I investigated. We got a call that a prehistoric bird was eating a cow in one of the fields not far from here. We got a lot of calls about similar things, from different people on different days. So I was dispatched in my police cruiser to investigate.

"What I saw was fascinating but at the same time frightening. There was this bird, wing-span about eight to ten feet, on the back of this cow, and not a small cow. So I got out of my car and walked into the field. I got close enough to take a picture of the action, and, as I got close, the bird flew away. An amazing sight. The cow seemed all right. The bird, it turned out was an egret, a large bird that feeds in ponds and marshes and rivers. Big birds, very big, but not prehistoric. But this one was unnaturally big. And it wasn't eating or attacking the cow. It was actually eating the insects and bugs that were on the cow's back. Can you see how a story can take on a life of its own, or how legends are born?" We began walking again. "Careful, that's poison ivy over there," I said. "Now, that plant over there is called a lady slipper."

"Yeah," he said. "I can tell by its shape."

"It's an endangered plant."

"Really?"

"Yeah, can't pick it. You'll get fined or arrested or worse," I told him.

As we headed back toward the school, he began to ask me questions. I would stop and study his face at times. I saw intelligence in his eyes, and I heard interest in his voice.

"Tony," I said, "let me tell you something about me. When I'm not here at the school, I am a college professor, and you know what makes students successful in high school and in college?"

"No," he said, and I no longer felt any resistance.

"Adaptability. Do you know what that means?"

"No, not really."

"Didn't think so. Remember the tadpoles we just saw?"

"Yup."

"Well, not all of them get eaten. Some hide and swim deep enough so that they're safe. They adapt and they survive. Ever read a fortune cookie?"

"Of course," he said.

"Well, here is a little fortune-cookie philosophy. You are no different than any other boy or girl in this school. The ones who seem cool are learning to adapt. The ones who look a little lost, sort of like you, my friend, are the tadpoles. Adapt or get swallowed up. Now, what do you think I would like you to do?"

He grinned. "Adapt."

"Good man. We'll work on that together. Deal?"

"Deal."

"We're all set," I told the principal when we returned to her office. "I'm going to take Tony up to his last period class."

A few days later, his teacher came down and handed me a written report Tony had turned in.

"I didn't assign this." She actually beamed. "Tony just did it on his own."

I gave the essay a glance, all the while trying to hide my grin. "On turtles?"

"Yes, and it's damn good. Read the first sentence."

It said: Turtles are terrestrial creatures; turtles that live on space ships are extraterrestrial turtles.

"Where did he get that from, Jack?"

"Don't know. Smart kid, though," I said. "How's he doing with the other kids?"

"He seems to be getting along," she said. "In fact, he's been talking a blue streak."

Later, I checked further on his progress. A pattern seemed to be developing. He was becoming more engaged with his classmates. As days went by, his teachers continued to report on his overall improvement.

Here was a kid who'd shut down. I could see he was heading nowhere. At first, he would not converse with anyone. But after our long walk that day, something had evidently clicked in his head. The trick was to establish a sense of trust. Without it, barriers could not be broken down—walls of resistance that prevented the exchange of mutually beneficial ideas. I say that because I always took something away from my walks, new lessons learned. I knew the turtles were out, and I thought it was worth a try to show him what I'd learned about them and their habitat. Often, these kids who go silent just need some space.

Sometimes, a simple change of environment, even a snapping turtle and a guy with a scar on his finger, can get a kid back on track.

CHAPTER 28

Caitlin: The Fury

If you'd asked me back then, if what healed Tony could heal Caitlin, I would have told you no way—and I would have been right. Caitlin's story broke my heart at times, and on other occasions, it gave me hope. Then there were the many other times she pissed me off, royally.

Caitlin was another school-choice kid. The reasons these students switched schools varied, but the most prevalent requests came from parents who were dissatisfied with their kid's present school.

Those accepted in the School Choice Plan had to pay tuition. This fee ensured that the program could hire top notch teachers and experienced staff members. The program enabled us to offer the most disenfranchised student a second chance.

One such troubled kid was Caitlin. She was a handful. More than a handful, she'd acted up so much as a thirteen-year-old that the faculty of her former school wanted her expelled. Our school was asked to be an alternative choice, which meant that here at the new school, we'd see if we could keep Caitlin headed in the right academic direction. She showed up as a sophomore, dressed in clean but grunge-looking clothes. She was five-foot-two and stocky, with Irish red hair. I'd already contacted the school resource officer from the other school for information.

"She's very defiant," her former SRO told me. "Fighting with girls, smoking in the bathroom, and walking out of detention. Explosive like a firecracker, Jack."

I knew middle school could be rough on kids, even fairly well-grounded ones.

The day she arrived, I made sure that I shook her hand and introduced myself. "If you need anything, I'm here for you," I told her.

"I would never talk to you." She stepped back and began to cower away from me. "I don't trust you, and I don't like you."

I didn't push the issue. "Okay, Caitlin," I said.

What a perfect way to get kicked out of a new school on your first day, I thought, *by pissing off one of the biggest authority figures these halls provide.* But this wasn't the first time I'd seen such behavior.

Later, I'd have cause to measure her high level of fear toward men. How real was it?

It eventually became apparent to me that she exhibited the characteristics seen in rape survivors. I had trained in rape investigations and had attended classes on adolescent self-destruction, so I had some basic understanding of emotional triggers.

Never would she meet my eyes during one of our meetings. She'd become an expert at totally dismissing me, telling me often that she didn't like me. In fact, she told me that she hated all her male teachers. Her mother, during consultations, would try to calm her down, but nothing worked. We, in the School Choice Program, could have asked her to leave, but we didn't.

Caitlin was assigned to the Zoo, and I didn't hear much about her for a couple of days. Then I spotted her crying in the guidance counselor's office. I did my best to comfort her, but she refused to acknowledge me. I backed off and conferred with her counselor, Peggy Carlyle.

Out of the young girl's earshot, Peggy shook her head and gave me a look I'd become used to seeing. "Jack," she said, "the other girls have started an avalanche on Facebook. Stuff about her being a whore and a slut."

"Jesus," I said, "already?"

"Word is she's been raped. Sadly, that brought all the crap to the surface at her other school."

"And transferred it here."

"Like wildfire," she said. "Think we can get to her?"

"I'm going to give it a shot," I said, not knowing where to start.

I approached Caitlin slowly, like a spider to a fly, pulling a chair over next to her and waiting. I knew she was living in her own personal hell, in her own world of self-blame, pointing fingers, and hushed voices. This was how other rape victims had described their feelings to me. With her, I got nothing but a pair of cold eyes.

"I can understand why you don't want to talk to me," I said. "If you want to pull up your Facebook, I'll take care of it."

She was hesitant. Maybe I was seeing things, but her eyes changed. "You can't do anything."

"Yes, I can. And if you have any problems here, you can come to me."

She began sobbing, that raw, heaving kind of crying that I knew came from feeling beaten. In talking to her mother before she came to the school, I'd learned she'd been bullied mercilessly. And now it was happening again. Whatever hope she'd been holding onto that it would be better at a new school had been ripped away from her.

I did my best to help her. But she had locked herself up again.

The next few days, she caused all the hell she could. She'd fight other girls at the slightest word, look, or other imagined gesture she thought was aimed at her. She was a fighter, waiting for an opponent. Anyone would do. If something bothered her in class, she simply walked out. Often, I was called to go find her.

One day, I spotted her slipping into the girls' room.

At my knock, she yelled, "I don't have any clothes on. Don't come in here."

I'd heard that before. "Cut the shit, Caitlin," I said. "I'll give you ten seconds to come out."

She came out and started to head for her class. When she veered left, away from the stairs, I grabbed her arm, nudging her in the right direction. "Your class is in 302, upstairs.

She kicked my shin. "Don't fucking touch me," she screamed.

This went on for five minutes. People started peeking out of doors. More gathered on the stairs going up and coming down. Meanwhile, my captive was moving like an Irish step dancer in a cage. I knew better than to touch a kid who'd become this emotional. Still, I didn't want her to hurt herself. Christ, I think she'd have jumped out of an open window if she could have found one.

That was when I saw our principal approaching me from the rear. Nick Mayhew, the assistant principal, rushed alongside her.

Ten minutes later, the three of us were standing in the main office, our faces flushed from dealing with Caitlin and the melee of kibitzers.

"What the hell happened?" Big Nick asked me. "Did you touch her?"

"Touch isn't the right word here, and yes, but not like that. Here's the thing, Nick, police officers use what is called a use-of-force continuum. Simply, that means we use very low force initially, like grabbing someone's elbow—that's called an "escort stance," meant to direct someone this way or that. But, when I grabbed her by the elbow she squirmed away, slippery little kid."

"But okay, you did touch her?"

"Nick, you're missing the big picture here. I didn't touch her. I was trying to redirect her, head her back in the right direction, toward the class she had just run from." I tried to put my rationalization into an understandable safety context. I'd been on this side of the fence before and I knew that, in the moment, it took a few minutes for questions and emotions to level off and for reason to take hold.

There was a big difference between educational, disciplinary, and actual touching. Educational touching is intended to gently guide a student in a specific direction, but it needs to be preceded by a verbal request and, in Caitlin's case, she reacted like a trapped beast, defensive and angry.

Now, if I'd chosen to use actual force, deciding that Caitlin's behavior was about to create a disturbance, then I would have grabbed her, controlled her, and handcuffed her in the same way police officers arrest a violent person on the street. Now, we were in a school so discretion on my part was the better part of valor.

"Did you go in the girls' restroom?" Kristin asked.

"No Kristen, I didn't," I said, holding my tongue.

I knew that her questions were coming from her ideas about liability, perception, and uninformed responses from happenstance witnesses. On occasions like this I was reminded that I was on loan to the school district, but I was a *police officer* on loan to the school district, a fact that didn't need clarification.

"Look," I said. "At first glance, this episode might look bad. But what's important is what actually happened." I knew this because some rape survivors had strong, internalized defense mechanisms. A screaming accusation of an improper touching was high on that list.

The following day, I found the bank of video tapes I needed. The police department had a lot of input in the school's choice of security cameras. They resembled those used in Vegas casinos' eye-in-the-sky cameras, only smaller. Most of the time, we had them pointed at every stairwell and back door. The camera I wanted was actually aimed at the hall in question.

After finding the video tape I was looking for, I invited Nick to watch it with me in Kristen's office. "There is Caitlin," I pointed out. "There she is walking into the girls' room."

The video now showed me at the lavatory's door. You couldn't hear me calling Caitlin's name, but you could see that I hadn't crossed the room's threshold. And soon the girl stormed through the door.

"Look at her, she's an adrenaline-powered pogo stick. See how she's jumping and screaming," I said. "And you can see how I tried to reason with her." I stopped the tape. "Look at her kicking me. For a police response, my actions were mild, trust me on that. Grabbing her was a very low response on the use-of-force continuum."

"What?" he asked.

"Nothing. Police talk, that's all," I said. "When I grabbed her by the arm coming out of the girls' room, and she started screaming, other officers might have slammed her on the ground and handcuffed her. Or they might have tried to discredit her. I just let her get it out, let her jump up and down. I wasn't going to play into the tantrum. Just saying that I touched her could get me fired."

The principal later invited me to show the tape to Caitlin and her mother in the principal's office. If it had been another regular student, she would have been sent home for her actions. We tried to talk about why her behavior was unacceptable.

"I have better things to do than look for you, Caitlin," I said. "Can you share some insights?"

She glared at me. "Fuck you. Don't touch me. Please don't touch me." Those words were branded on the young girl's indelible soul and shot out her mouth on instinct.

I could have stayed, but my presence was keeping them from being able to talk to her. Later that day, the mother came upstairs to my office and filled me in on her daughter.

"Sit down," I told her. "And let's talk."

It wasn't easy for her. It never was when they really wanted to talk about their kid and not themselves. "Caitlin was fourteen." She asked for water and I quickly provided it for her. "Her uncle raped her. When we tried to confront him, he said she was a lying bitch and a whore. He never touched her, he said. There was an investigation. They charged him with statutory rape, indecent assault, and battery on a minor."

I allowed her a moment to compose herself. "Anyone under the age of sixteen is considered a juvenile," I said, hoping to start the conversation up again.

She managed to go on. "I didn't report it right away," she said. "And, of course..." She began to cry softly.

"So, no rape kit was done?"

"No," she said. "It was his word against Caitlin's."

I asked the tough question in the way I'd learned to. "And you believed your daughter?"

"I did."

"And your husband, others in the family?"

"Her father hasn't been involved. We've been divorced for years. George is a skinny, squirrely type, kind of a strange guy. But no one thought he'd ever rape his own niece."

I learned that she'd hired an attorney and had accused Mr. Squirrel of accosting her child. There had been signs of abuse in her history folder, and now this woman had made it clear how she and Caitlin had been suffering. There were so many kids that had that little asterisk in their folders. Many grew through it. But with this girl, the wounds were still fresh.

Once I'd talked to her mother, Caitlin's behavior began to make sense. The screaming was a defense mechanism from post-traumatic stress. It served the purpose of bringing other people to her.

The day after one of the court hearings, she and two other girls came into my office.

"What can I do for you, ladies?" I said, happy that Caitlin had reached the point where she would talk to me.

"What does an arraignment mean?" she asked then looked at a notebook she'd drawn from her backpack. "What does discovery mean?"

I explained to her that I had testified many times in court. I kind of walked her through what a rape trial was like.

"You have to be careful with your outbursts," I warned her. "There are going to be people who try to portray you negatively. Court is like the theater and you have to play your role completely. You're the victim. Don't let anyone tell you anything differently."

I don't think she'd ever heard anything like that before. She'd evidently had so many fingers pointed at her, a feeling of guilt had entered her mind.

"You have to act like a victim, and you have to be nicely dressed. When he's in the courtroom, you meet his eyes, and you stare at the jury. They're going to be watching your body language. No swearing or giving people the finger."

It was the first time she had come to me for help. I knew these other girls. I was sure they had convinced her to come and see me. She never would have done that alone. I felt she was letting her guard down a little. The next time she visited me without the girl guards.

With girls, I never shut my door.

We would talk about her court appearances. We'd talk, but nothing really deep. I would just answer her questions. Instead of hiding when she walked out of class, she'd visit me.

"Caitlin," I'd say, "where are you supposed to be?"

"English."

"Did you just walk out of class?"

"I needed some fresh air."

I'd call the teacher. "Caitlin is with me. I had an appointment with her and forgot to give her a slip."

The trial ended with a hung jury.

Juries are unpredictable. Courts can be perplexing. She didn't take the stand on my advice, and I was sure her attorneys didn't want her to either. Sometimes, jurors sympathize with the defendant. I'm sure his lawyers had painted Mr. Squirrel as someone who had fallen on hard times. The court is really not about justice. It's about who is more convincing in the theater that is happening live.

Caitlin was relieved when it was over, even though it was a hung jury. It's often said that in the halls of justice, justice happens in the halls: plea bargains, restitution, winks, nods, and promises. In my experience, victims get the short end of the stick. The scales don't always tilt in their favor.

She was my pal after that. She started to blend. It was about getting to that point, as it was with a lot of other kids. They were using my office as a way to waste time. I'd just write them a pass and tell them to make the like trees and leave. When I had time for them, they could stay and talk to me. If I was busy, I would just send them on their way.

"You need to be in the classroom," I'd say when all they wanted was a break.

Everything seemed to be going well for Caitlin. She still had tantrum behavior, but she and I were forming a mutual friendship. She knew I'd never lie to her, and we talked about everything.

A couple of months later, she stopped coming to school. She had mononucleosis and the teachers were sending her homework home.

Then I got a call from the school district she'd transferred from. The SRO at that school greeted me with, "Jack, little Caitlin?"

"What'd she do?"

"She got raped, teen-dating violence this time—boyfriend I think."

Just like that. Everything fell off the earth.

Apparently one night at a party, a bunch of kids had been drinking and her boyfriend wouldn't take no for an answer. He beat her pretty badly. It wasn't mono that was keeping her out of school. She stayed home for the remainder of the school year. She did her homework, enough that she advanced to the next grade. I called her mother, but she didn't want to talk to me.

I had a debriefing meeting with the crisis team, and we talked about what we might do for this kid. I even had the police report from the second rape that the SRO in her town had faxed me. She had been transported to the hospital that night, and they did do a rape kit for her. There was no doubt this time that it had actually occurred. This time, they had the proof.

And this time, she eventually came to me for help. She was in my office every day. It was like an unspoken bond, and I was her friend.

"You know why I like you, Officer Hobson," she asked while we were taking a walk around the school grounds. She didn't wait for me to answer. "You always have my back."

"What do you mean?"

"You haven't told anyone about me."

"Why would I? If you want to tell people, you can."

"But you do ask to see my homework."

"You know how I feel about homework."

She took a piece of paper and printed an acronym on it. *H-O-M-E-W-O-R-K. Half Of My Education Wasted On Random Knowledge.*

She and her friends would answer the phone in my office when they could beat me to it. "Officer Hobson's office," they'd say. When it was my wife, Nancy, Caitlin would chat with her. She seemed pretty cheerful.

Then she seemed to shut down again. The rape trial was coming up. I asked my superiors at the station about it. The boy was being tried a couple of towns over.

I went to the superior court and sat in the courtroom in uniform for no other reason than that she could see me. It would make her smile, and she would relax a little bit. I did that the first four days of the trial.

They made a plea deal with the rapist. He'd be convicted, and it looked like he would do seven to ten years. He ended up serving four, if that.

You could see her change of attitude.

"You don't know how much it helped our family with you being in court," the mother said.

"I like Caitlin, and she's coming back to school. If she gets in any other trouble, at least we can take care of it quickly."

When she was sixteen, I signed a work certificate for her so that she could go to work at a fast food place. When I retired, she was a senior. When I was in and out of the hospital, she and her friends sent me cards and wrote notes to me.

Then she dropped out of school. I was home recovering when the guidance counselor called me and gave me the news.

I tried calling her back but got her voice mail.

"Caitlin, call me," I said. "You're not in trouble. I'm feeling fine and I want to talk to you."

She called right away, crying. She said she just couldn't take the rumors after the rape trial.

"Get into the alternative high school."

"I can't get in."

"Caitlin, I'm on the board of directors," I said. "Will you go?"

I made a phone call and got her into the school. I paid her tuition. Nobody asked why. She was in a crowd of kids where she could talk and be herself and actually learn.

She eventually went back to school and graduated. I was the keynote speaker for her graduation. She was in the front row. That whole class was made up of kids that one way or another had their lives affected by me.

ജ୬ଙ

A Speech and a Song:

"Good morning, graduates, family, friends, teachers, and those only here for the free lobster rolls and cake. I love cake!

"You're probably wondering what I am going to talk about, and I'll tell you. About ten minutes." Applause. "As I scan the audience, I see some old friends, bright-eyed and full of pride. Old nemeses that made my school resource officer days interesting and perplexing and, at times, hectic. Diamonds in the rough. I remember a young man who threw an apple in the café one day, and the apple struck an unsuspecting diner in the face, chipping her tooth. But I won't name names. Is that all right with you, David?"

"Sure, Jack. It's cool."

"I'm proud of you, man! Wow, fifteen success stories: Seize the day, my friends. Hey Liam, my man, what does your tattoo say?"

"*Carpe diem.*"

"And what does that mean?"

"Seize the day," he said.

"Exactly," I said with a smile. "Good morning, Michael. Let me ask you a question. Oh, I remember. How much does spray paint cost?"

"About ten dollars."

"That's about right. My friend, Michael, was quite a graffiti artist."

"A Rembrandt, Officer Hobson. I was the man," he replied.

"You were something, all right. I see you hiding, Laura."

"Oh God. Please, Jack, don't."

"Laura didn't have the word 'patience' in her vocabulary and as a result, she couldn't wait until she was seventeen to get a driver's license, so she borrowed her Dad's pick-up truck and decided to take a nice drive in the country. Only problem was she didn't understand the concept of a stop sign or what to do when a police car is behind you with lights and sirens blaring. How lucky you were that the police officer was me."

The audience continued to laugh. "Hey, Lenny, is that you up there in the cheap seats? Not trying to avoid me, are you?"

"No way, Officer Hobson," he said in a trembling voice.

"Are you hungry, Lenny?"

"You mean right now?"

"Sure, right now," I said.

"Yeah, I'm starving."

He was always in a perpetual state of hunger. Laughter broke out, mostly among the graduates, because they all knew that Lenny was their resident stoner in school, now the stoner emeritus after graduation.

"Let me ask you this. What food do you think best resembles your personality? What best describes you?"

"Do I have to say it, Jack?" he pleaded.

I nodded feverishly.

"I'm a soup-sandwich."

"Can't hear you, Lenny."

"I am a soup sandwich!"

Laughter continued.

"Wouldn't care to share that recipe, would you?"

"No, not really. No," he said.

I heard soft inquiries from the parents in front rows. "Did he call him a tuna sandwich?'

"No a soup sandwich."

"A what? What's a soup sandwich? How can soup…"

"You're a good man, Lenny, and today you are a graduate, your reign as being King of the Soup-Sandwiches ends today. Does that work for you?'

"Thanks, Jack. It works just fine."

"Jeffrey, you look very dapper today. Did you dress yourself? I always felt bad for young Mr. Wells here because during his high school years, the only clothes he had was a dirty stocking hat and baggy shorts. He was the only person on the planet who actually had a skateboard surgically attached to his body. Let's see…who haven't I greeted on this very important and reverent day?"

I made eye contact with an old member of my dark knight's club. "Marcus, how are you, my *compadre*? Now understand that my man Marcus here was quite a track star, fast runner, and quite the adventurer. Take a deep breath, Marc. This won't take long," I said with a smile.

"Okay, one day, Marcus was very hungry, famished, but he had no money for food, so he borrowed a few hotdogs and a meatball sub. I was in the cafeteria when a lunch lady told me about his descent into his very brief life of crime. When I confronted him, he ran, full-out sprint, down the hallway, out the door, and into the woods that surround the school. As an old-school cop, there was no way I was going to chase him. A short time later, I began to hear yelling, a plea for help echoing from the woods. I grabbed my binoculars and searched for the origin of the screams. I saw Marcus, tough to miss in his orange hoodie sweatshirt, standing upright but snagged within a briar patch. He was rescued, brought to the nurse. End of story? Not really, but only we know the rest of that story. Right, my friend?"

"Thanks, Officer Hobson. That was a very nice story."

"Oh, the pleasure was all mine. And, one more thing, Marc, and I'll say this quietly so only you and I can hear. If you have to go to jail, think big, hit an armored car. Don't go to jail for a day-old hot dog. *Capisci*? That's Italian for do you understand."

Slouching in his seat, he said, "It's all good, Officer Hobson, I mean, Jack."

"Okay, almost done," I said. "Good morning, Caitlin."

"Good morning, Jack" she said with a bite in her tone.

If looks could kill, I thought.

"Just so everyone understands, Caitlin and I are good friends. We've helped each other out many times, and although I'm not an SRO anymore, we keep in touch, and it's always good to talk with her. One story, Caitlin, I promise. But which one? There are so many. The day Caitlin entered high school she was, let's say, a bit hostile, vocal, and wild—like a captured lioness, wild. She escaped from her first class and was running freely up and down the halls. I was tasked to find her and bring her to the principal's office. I found her, grabbed her arm to prevent another escape, when she kicked me in the shin, scratched my arm, and was loose once more. Enough said. I'm proud of you, Caitlin."

She got up from the first row and gave me a hug. The laughter drowned out the applause.

ૡૐૡ

I wasn't quite done with my speech, I needed to hook up an iPod and equalize the speakers, but I had time to reflect a bit. Caitlin had new friends now, and she had some degree of closure. People now believed her. Here was a girl who had been abused and had managed to go forward. She told me she hated school and was ready to drop out, but she wanted to come see me and talk. As we grew closer as friends, I would constantly tell her that the sky was the limit and that her success was only limited by her imagination.

Before I left the stage, I told the graduating class that "Vienna waits for you." I told them *Vienna* was a Billy Joel song and that if they listened closely to the lyrics, they would know how I felt about them and what great things life had in store for them. I asked the graduation class if they knew the song and its meaning, and nobody did. So, armed with my iPod and speakers, I asked the assembled, my diamonds in the rough, to close their eyes and listen." And I made it a point to say "Caitlin, my friend, this song's for you." Actually, it was a homage to the whole class.

I saw tears in Caitlin's eyes and, at that point, I knew she would be fine. She'd find her wings, I was sure of it. In conclusion, I said what I always said, and I said it with pride and conviction.

"*Shine on You Crazy Diamonds.*" – Pink Floyd, September 15, 1974, London.

CHAPTER 29

Passages

*Anyone can become angry. That is easy.
But to be angry with the right person,
to the right degree, at the right time,
for the right purpose and in the right way—
that is not easy.* – Aristotle

The greatest victory requires no battle. – Sun Tzu

At the moment of Caitlin's graduation, I couldn't imagine any other life than standing before and with those kids, supporting them, dishing out tough love when necessary, and, overall, being the person who kept them from drifting too far. What the kids didn't know, and what I did my best to deny, was that I was dealing with a silent enemy.

For ten years, I had struggled with a disease that attacked my colon and stomach. I'd had minor surgery that appeared so simple, an outpatient procedure, followed by a few weeks out of work. And then it happened, a hiccup. Complications led to other corrective surgeries. One after the other, every six months for four years. I found myself weak, physically and emotionally. Days turned into weeks that turned into months of working in pain, with high fevers, dragging myself and an ileostomy with me, all the time being told by doctors that my next procedure would be my last.

Life decisions, agonizing ones, were made for me. At one time, I was always thinking ahead, planning, looking to the future, in control. Now, I walked a tightrope, without a net, over perilous waters.

After a career that spanned thirty-three years, I hit the wall and came face-to-face with the callous side of the culture I had been part of. I became, not Jack the asset, but Jack the nuisance.

Obviously in poor health and struggling to improve, I could no longer fake it. Money and budgets and dollars and cents trumped empathy. "It's not personal, Jack. It's just business," I was told.

On the contrary, having a three-decade career reduced to subtle threats about using sick time and about how the department could not "carry me" anymore sounded personal. Being filleted in public before my peers felt very personal—those in charge forgetting the human side of the equation. A new administration flexing its muscles, stroking its ego at the expense of others, attacking, and taking advantage of the weak because they could. Where was the fabled brotherhood, you know, that powerful, unbreakable bond. It never materialized.

I morphed into a budget problem, more of a villain than a person in need of assistance. There was no helping hand, only the hands that held the axe. And in time, it fell. I was no longer psychologically safe. I felt abandoned, and I was frightened.

Police culture can be intense and fickle, judgmental and secretive. Dangerous and unforgiving. Clannish and unpredictable. It can be nurturing, or it can blitz with reckless abandon. The thin blue line shifts and drifts, controlled by those in higher positions and those who want to *be* in high positions. Friendship and the protection it provides are thinly veiled misconceptions.

The casual and callous indifference toward me hurt the most.

I no longer identified with others who wore the same uniform. They no longer considered me one of them. I became, like many of my Zoo friends, a broken toy. I was in uncharted territory, and I learned at fifty-five years old, that not only delinquents drift. So do adults.

I needed a radical transition. I needed to start a new chapter, the next part of my life, and I was ready.

One day, my wife, Nancy, returned home to see me working in the yard.

"What are you doing here?" she asked.

"I retired," I told her. "It was like a light suddenly illuminated inside my head. It was time."

She sat on the porch for a long time, contemplating the future and struggling with the reality that the future was now. When she came in, she had accepted my decision. She knew it was coming because we had discussed it at length, but on the day I left, I knew I could no longer wait. It was my time.

That was July of 2011.

༂༃༂

That was then and this is now. I had worked hard and long to improve myself and to bring common sense, patience, experience, and humility to the school and to the students I worked with and for.

I had sacrificed a great deal to achieve my goals, both professionally and academically. With grace and strength, my wife was there to hold down the fort and hold my hand. She was and is my support system.

Now, I'm a Visiting Associate Professor of Criminal Justice at a major university south of Boston. My doctorate in education gives me the best of both academic worlds. I teach a variety of courses, and for the first time in a long time, I'm content and happy.

During a recent Ethics in Criminal Justice class, I facilitated a discussion about the legalization of medical marijuana.

As students talked and debated, I wrote their rapid-fire opinions, pro and con, on the blackboard. Two students dominated the discussion. It was an intellectual tug-of-war, the best kind of class.

I stressed that they must narrow their focus, break down a topic into its intricate parts and strive to create a forensic discussion. "Forensic," I told them. "It's Greek for forum."

Brandy, one of my former students from high school, took the legalization side. Her premise was that marijuana was an herb and, as such, natural. When compared to alcohol, it was less addictive, and when used as a stress reliever or to ease pain, it was second to none. She did an excellent job in narrowing her focus.

The con side was articulated by a student citing the addictive properties of marijuana, its role as a gateway drug, and its legalization akin to a scourge on society. As I wrote on the blackboard, I asked him how he formed his opinions. He said he learned them in high school from his DARE officer.

"Really? Your DARE officer. You must have been paying attention," I said.

"I was, Officer Hobson," he replied.

I paused, turned, and faced the class. He had said *Officer Hobson*, not professor or Dr. Hobson, but *officer*. "I was your DARE officer?"

"Yes," and as he said that, another hand waved in class.

"What's up, Brandy?" I said.

"You were my DARE officer, too."

"I knew that," I said.

"And you honestly don't recognize Alex?" she asked.

Embarrassed, I said, "No, not really."

"He was, like, in your office every day."

"I remember *you* were, like, in my office every day." To the boy, I said, "What's your last name?"

"It's me—Alex—you know the kid you terrorized in high school," he said.

I searched my memory. Then I was stunned. "Little Alex from the zoo," I said as the class laughed.

"I've been here for ten sessions now," he said. "You didn't recognize me?"

"No, Alex, I didn't. I'm sorry. I'm just an absent-minded professor with two brains. One's lost and other one is looking for it." It was a weak defense and I knew it.

"You used to say that to me all the time and to everyone else." He laughed. "You also used to tell me that I had bad etiquette, and that I was a numbskull."

"Knucklehead," I said. "Okay, class dismissed." I waved them out. "Come on, Alex. You can buy me a coffee."

He grinned. "Cool beans."

"How's your mother, is she still…"

"A little bat-shit crazy?" He chuckled. "She wants to e-mail you. Would that be okay?"

"Absolutely," I said. "Let's take a walk around campus and catch up."

He nodded. "Still walking with students, Officer Hobson." A statement more than a question.

"All the time," I said. "It helps me think."

EPILOGUE

Now What?

Aschool shooting. It can happen anywhere, in any town, in any city. No community is immune. No school is protected against every evil contingency. Evil knows no boundaries.

On Friday, December 14, 2012 at 9:30 in the morning, evil visited the Sandy Hook Elementary School in Newtown, Connecticut.

It happened quickly and senselessly in a small New England town that, in less than a minute, became part of the American consciousness. Twenty first-grade children were murdered. But victims are ageless. On December 14, teachers became heroes in death.

Now what?

The shooter is dead. The number of victims is horrifying. A community in shock, a country outraged and grieving, Newtown, Connecticut was added to the list of tragic iconic violence, one more set of statistics in an improbable equation.

I wish I could tell you I'm an expert on school violence. I'm not convinced that there are any experts. I wrote a dissertation about it. I teach prevention strategies. I talk about suspects and victims and their correlation.

The numbers tell us very little except a death toll, bullets fired, and interactions with victims. Date, time of day, duration of the assault, statistics, and equations. Forensics and psychology attempt to explain behavior, pinpoint a cause, but empirical evidence cannot rationalize its aftereffects. There is no crystal ball. No magic potion of prevention. But diligence increases awareness, awareness heightens our senses, and that can lessen the odds for violence.

It's a sad reality, but some things in life are not predictable and subsequently not judiciously preventable. School violence is one of them. Car crashes are another. Some crashes are not survivable, even when the best safety equipment is used.

I knew there was a good chance that I could not stop the first shot inside my school. As an SRO, I walked my school armed and in full uniform. I wore a bullet-proof vest. I kept extra vests in my office to offer protection or to shield an injured victim. I did radio tests. Just as important, I listened to the sounds of the building, filtering out the normal everyday chatter, listening for a sudden change of inflection. Angry tones, raised voices. Emotions manifest in a cacophony of loud and rapid sounds. And emotions are mimicked as the sounds become coordinated. That's fear. I watched for unusual movement. I was observant and on guard, prepared.

We cannot turn schools into fortresses or prisons. We can't allow teachers or other employees to carry guns, but we need to restrict gun laws concerning automatic weapons. And, let's embrace new ideas about school safety, but not at the expense of students. Having said that, I don't agree with the idea of training students to mount an attack, to go on the offensive, bring the fight to the attacker. I don't think children are psychologically equipped to handle the blood and gore of a school shooting and its after-effects. Many of the children, that would be trained, probably sleep with a nightlight on, for fear of the boogey-man or the green hand under the bed. Combat training, really? Children should not be taught to think and react like a soldier. We're not in Yemen. How about meticulous record checks on individuals before they can buy a gun? Oh, I know—it's too expensive, and the manpower costs would be astronomical. Interesting how we can reduce owning and carrying a firearm to dollars and cents and then wrap the flag around the second amendment. School safety is expensive, too. And school safety and firearms are not synonymous.

The right to keep and bear arms. It's a simple statement, but a complex philosophy. The second amendment is not intended to be the cornerstones of a right-wing prophecy, in which a safe society equates to everyone shouldering an assault rifle. But for many, it is and the prophets are telling the faithful to buy large weapons, more powerful than those carried by our enemies, our domestic antagonists, the cowards that invade our schools and kill our children. If that were the only reason, the paramount and central idea about our responses to tragedies like Newtown and many others, I'd agree. But is access to high-caliber, automatic weapons the answer? Do the criminally insane really care what they're up against? Where will the next tragic school event happen? When the time to act comes, the time to prepare is past.

So we train and plan and dissect current tragedies to prevent future violence. We need to do a better job. A word to the politicians: funeral directors are rich enough.

I understand that even in schools that have modern security and SROs, there is a real possibility that the first shot cannot be stopped, but perhaps through better communication, the second, third, or twentieth shot *can* be stopped.

Ban the sale of assault rifles and automatic weapons. Increase communication. Replace batteries. Run daily radio tests. Practice drills. Talk openly about current events and find teachable moments within social media and pop culture. Stop whispering about consequences. The truth makes the strongest foundation. Talk about precautions and plans to prevent violence. Bring children into the conversation. Listen to their concerns. Act upon them and let them know you did. That's critical for information transference, understanding, and cooperation. Sustain or improve the climate of the school. Be positive and reassuring. Be patient with children. Be patient with yourself.

There is nothing new in school security. Sure, there's new technology, but it cannot replace human intuition and observation. Technology is not sensory. Not yet. It has no pulse. Allow commonsense to merge with concrete policies and procedures. Reevaluate, re-train, and recertify everyone: janitors, nurses, secretaries, volunteers. Every adult has a stake in the school, but never lose sight of the fact that civilians are not police officers. Talk about proactive initiatives and where each person fits into its puzzle. Initiate an understandable chain of command.

Police train to minimize casualties. Police officers and SROs are trained to confront the threat with deadly force or with their own lives, if necessary. I would have. I walked my entire school many times a day. Checked doors. Checked cars parked conspicuously. Talked with students about their perception of rumors.

Assist the school with a threat assessment or security audit. A threat assessment is a behavioral study. A security audit looks for the proverbial weak links in a

security plan. Talk about and listen to faculty concerns—
they are first line of defense, their reactions focused on
the safety of their "kids." Help educators map out the
school, each door, windows, which way faces north,
south, east, and west. Post the map. Improve
communication. Walk the school with staff. Walk the
school with police officers and firemen. Even the most
basic information in a crisis can save lives. Check the
doors and exits less traveled. Understand that security
outside is as important as security inside. You can't have
one without the other.

The monster that invaded Sandy Hook Elementary
shot his way through the glass front door and, for him, it
was game on. He had a plan before he'd even arrived at
the building. Most do. The shooter knows how it will end
and has embraced the finale, his place in history. What he
may not know is how long he has. So the brutality is
immediate. The victims—wrong place, wrong time, in the
line of fire.

Improve communication.

The killers at Columbine were teased and ostracized.
We know that by their diaries. The murderer at Sandy
Hook was said to be mentally ill and paranoid.
Commonalities? Yes, access to weapons. Their states of
mind during the assault—elation shadowed by suicide.
We know this by interviews and statements from shooters
who survived and from victims and witnesses.
Everyone's a victim.

Can we profile a shooter? If time and circumstances
allow, but that would mean disrupting a plan. Psychosis
is rarely linear. Their motives appear to be revenge, and
revenge fantasies are a cornerstone of mental illness.

There is an old saying attributed to organized crime.
If you're going out to seek revenge, dig two graves. The
idea being that the assailant is not coming out alive, and

that he will occupy one grave. The other—size and depth notwithstanding—is merely an horrific metaphor for a mass grave. It's a between a rock and a hard place dilemma, a no win situation. Take no prisoners, as it were.

The problems of school violence are complex. The educator in me knows that we need to take a more focused look at depression in young males and understand the connections between violence and feelings of shame and injustice. There are so many ways to lose boys to violence. Checklists of warning signs, behavioral profiles, and threat assessments may be only first steps.

Other steps include scheduling regular debriefings with guidance counselors, psychologists, nurses—and any other people skilled in aberrant or strange behavior in students—noting changes in personalities, family conditions, and attendance. If anyone has an inkling about an upcoming event, a murder plot, or attack of any kind, tell someone. Tell two or three people. There is no time like the present to engage in an open conversation about at-risk students and their mental health.

Tomorrow is a new day.

Each morning, I welcomed and ushered hundreds of students into the school, and each afternoon, as the buses were taking them home, I breathed a little easier.

Postscript

Ten Minutes inside the Gates of Hell

Barely one hundred and twenty days after the Newtown tragedy, the City of Boston made that horrible list of places with epic violence, as two pressure-cooker bombs were detonated within the crowd watching runners as they raced to the finish line of the Boston Marathon. Mayhem struck at 2:29 p.m., Patriot's Day, Monday, April 15, 2013.

Instantly, after the first bomb exploded, there was an immediate communion of brave and defiant personalities. These people acted with a will that could not be broken, a visceral need to protect the living and care for the dead. With each rescue came a silent resolve to stand their ground more steadfastly than before.

The City of Boston is my second hometown. I grew up only miles from Boston's ground zero.

The accounts of this day and the stories of heroic feats are endless. Tales of amazing strength and grace under fire.

First responders, federal, state, and local law enforcement, as well as, military assets, worked as one, creating a wrecking crew of unstoppable momentum.

The evidence was quickly processed. The terrorists were tracked down. The capture was swift. The incident was over, the causalities beyond measure. For many, life without arms or legs or hearing and sight will always be a horrific reminder of the fateful day. But Boston breeds strong people with incorruptible spirits, resolves as strong as the strongest steel.

We all prayed for the victims. The world prayed for the victims.

I prayed hard for the youngest killed, an eight-year-old boy. About the same age as the Newtown children. A before photograph showed him smiling the way only little boys can smile, a little mischievous through chipped teeth with a twinkle in his eyes—such a hope-filled, magical innocence.

Just days before he died in the wake of the first explosion, the finish line bomb, he had created a poster, a fifth-grade school project in response to the well-publicized shooting incident in Florida, it read: *No more hurting people. Peace.*

It was inked in multi-colored magic markers on a poster board that now hangs in memoriam.

The truth is so simple, out of the mouth of babes. Rest in Peace, little man.

THINKING AHEAD

For Adults, parents, and those of us who still have that teenage spirit within us, I hope these stories are helpful and ground for continued discussion and critical thoughts about children and their *DRIFT*.

The thoughts about theory and individual behavior were my own, reinforced by textbooks and professional experience.

Most all of my misbehaving friends displayed symptoms of the larger issues that are associated with juvenile delinquency.

I dealt with their symptoms before the hurtful labeling and castigation became rooted and toxic.

As with any memoirs, I tried to spark certain experiences and recollections by reading specific articles and studies germane to my characters and individual stories about their behavior.

Gender aside, I tried, through the practical application of preemptive and restorative ideas, to seek out certain commonalities of delinquent behavior and to act upon them consistently—a struggle of cause and effect.

It is my hope that parents will find some useful dialogue within this book and talk to their children about all the clear and present dangers that exist today.

Remember, they're only children for a very short time. A blink and they're adults, with their own experiences, formative memories and perception of things, past and present.

Acknowledgements

Early in my quest to put my thoughts and police experiences to paper, I learned that writing was the easy part. It was fun, and my ideas flowed easily. Shortly after, there was professional interest in my work, I learned that a manuscript needed to be massaged, trimmed, pulled, and molded into something that makes sense and captures the attention of an audience.

A high five to Larry Leichman from Arbor Books, who listened patiently to the rant of a stranger before telling me that my story ideas were fun and relevant and not so farfetched.

It's hard to work in an organization for almost three decades without being impacted and indebted to some co-workers. For that I thank Chief George Gurley and Chief Bill Ferioli, two police chiefs who embraced the concept of community policing and afforded me the tools and resources to bring prevention initiatives into the schools and throughout the community. To my fellow police officers, young and old; there are so many, and too many to acknowledge, so please accept my thanks for making so many years of controlled chaos the experience of a lifetime.

As a police officer working to embrace community policing, beginning in the 1990s, my success and that of my police department was helped in no small way by the Plymouth County District Attorney's Office. Former District Attorney and former United States Attorney Mike Sullivan created a legacy of cooperation by joining with police officers in taking prevention education into the classroom. Taking the mantle from Mike Sullivan was D.A. Tim Cruz, who continued in the footsteps of others to make his office one of the most progressive and proactive allies supporting school-based officers. And special thanks to a long-time friend, dissertation advisor, and confederate on many adventures throughout academia and the halls of justice, Ed Jacoubs.

As a police officer assigned to the school district, I had to straddle two worlds. Bridging the gap between organizational cultures was no easy task, but I was embraced and welcomed into the school's fold by professionals ranging from janitors, cafeteria workers, teachers, guidance counselors, coaches, compassionate and proactive nurses, principals and their assistants— awesome assistants I might add—and so many others, from top to bottom, too many to name, but you know who you are.

And a big high five to Dr. Carolyn Petrosino, Ph.D from Bridgewater State University for penning my Forword. I am grateful for her friendship and her advice throughout the years.

I am grateful to the extraordinary people at Black Opal Books for taking me under their wings and having the faith that I could fly. To my editor Lauri Wellington, for walking the walk when it came to "telling the stories that needed to be told," my stories.

It's difficult to find the words to thank Bonnie Hearn Hill for her insight, patient direction and redirection; for being my friend, my critic, and my cheerleader. Bonnie, you fashioned me into something I had only dreamed of becoming. A writer. And for that, I am eternally grateful.

And to my cover designer, Christopher Allan Poe, whose talent was so spontaneous, so spot on, that all at once, Chris, you eased my stress about the cover, so I could stress about other things. Shine on, you crazy diamond.

Finally, and the truth of this salute borders on cliché, but if it weren't for my wife Nancy, not one of my personal and professional dreams could have come true. Twenty-five years ago she became my world and has never left my side. I haven't been the easiest child to handle, but it's all good now. This book, this labor of love is dedicated to her.

Resources

Aaron, L. &Dallaire, D.H. (2010), "Parental Incarceration and Multiple Risk Experiences: Effect on Family Dynamics and Children's Delinquency," *Journal of Youth and Adolescence*, 39(12), 1471-1484.

American Psychiatric Association (2010), *Diagnostic and Statistical Manual of Mental Disorders*, (4th ed., text revision).Washington, DC: Author.

American Psychiatric Association (2010), *DSM 5 Development: Conduct Disorder*, retrieved from: http://www. dsm5.org/ProposedRevision/Pages/proposedrevision.aspx ?rid=370Baker

Bartol, Curt & Bartol, Anne (2009), *Juvenile Delinquency and Antisocial Behavior: A Developmental Perspective*, (3rd ed.) Upper Saddle River, New Jersey: Pearson Prentice Hall.

Brown, S. (1998), *Understanding Youth and Crime (Listening to youth?)*, Buckingham: Open University Press. Page 109.

Coie, J. & Dodge, K. (1998), "Aggression and antisocial behavior," in W. Damon (Series Ed.) & N. Eisenberg (Vol. Ed.), *Handbook of child psychology: Vol.2. Social, emotional, and personality development*, (5th ed., pp.779-862), New York: Wiley.

Cullen, F. T., & Gendreau, P. (2000), "Assessing correctional rehabilitation: Policy, practice, and prospects," In J. Horney (Ed.), *NIJ criminal justice 2000: Changes in decision making and discretion in the criminal justice system*, (pp. 109–175), Washington, DC: U.S. Department of Justice, National Institute of Justice.

Cullen, F. T., Wright, J. P., & Chamlin, M. B, (1999), "Social support and social reform: A progressive crime control agenda," *Crime & Delinquency*, 45(2), 188–207.

Curtis, N. M., Ronan, K. R., & Borduin, C. M. (2004), "Multisystemic treatment: A meta-analysis of outcome studies," *Journal of Family Psychology*, 18(3), 411–419.

Dembo,R.,& Gulledge, L.M. (2009), "Truancy intervention programs: Challenges and innovations to implementation," *Criminal Justice Policy Review*, 20(4), 437–456.

Hinshaw, S. P., & Lee, S. S. (2003), "Conduct and oppositional defiant disorders," in E. J. Mash & R. A. Barkley (Eds.), *Child psychopathology*, (pp. 144-198), New York: Guilford Press.

Krohn, M., Hall, G.P., & Lizotte, A.J. (2009), "Family transitions and later delinquency and drug use," *Journal of Youth and Adolescence*, 38, 466–480.

Lahey, B. B., Miller, T. L., Gordon, R. A., & Riley, A. W. (1999), "Developmental epidemiology of the disruptive behavior disorders," in H. C. Quay & A. E. Hogan (Eds.), *Handbook of disruptive disorders*, (pp. 23-48). New York: Kluwer Academic/Plenum Publishers.

Laub, J. H., & Sampson, R. J. (2003), *Shared beginnings, divergent lives: delinquent boys to age 70*, Cambridge, Massachusetts: Harvard University Press.

Lehr, C. A., Hansen, A., Sinclair, M. F., & Christenson, S. L. (2003), "Moving beyond dropout towards school completion: An integrative review of data-based interventions," *School Psychology Review,* 32(3), 342–364.

Moffitt (2006), "Life course persistent versus adolescent limited antisocial behavior," in D. Cicchetti& D. Cohen (Eds.) *Developmental Psychopathy*, (2nd ed.) New York: Wiley.

Murray J; Farrington DP (Oct 2010), "Risk factors for conduct disorder and delinquency: key findings from longitudinal studies," *Can J Psychiatry*, 55 (10): 633-42, PMID20964942.

Murrihy, R., Kidman, A., & Ollendick, T. (2010), *Clinical Handbook of Assessing and Treating Conduct Problems in Youth*, Springer: New York.

Sampson, R. J., & Laub, J. H. (2005), "A general age-graded theory of crime: Lessons learned and the future of life-course criminology," in D. P. Farrington (Ed.) *Integrated developmental & life course theories of offending: Advances in criminological theory*, (Volume 14) (pp. 165–182), New Brunswick, New Jersey: Transaction.

Siegel, Larry J. and Brandon Welsh, *Juvenile Delinquency: The Core*, (4th ed.) Belmont, California: Wadsworth/ Cengage Learning, 2011.

Steinberg, L. (2008), *Adolescence*, (8th ed.) New York, New York: McGraw-Hill.

"Study Reveals Specific Gene in Adolescent Men with Delinquent Peers," *Newswise*, retrieved on October 1, 2008.

U.S. Department of Justice, (2006), *Psychiatric disorders of youth in detention*, (NCJ 210331) Washington, DC: U.S. Government Printing Office.

Violence by Teenage Girls: Trends and Context, Office of Justice Programs, U.S. Department of Justice

Welsh, B.C. (2003), "Economic costs and benefits of primary prevention of delinquency and later offending: A review of the research" in D.P. Farrington and J.W., Coid (eds) *Early prevention of adult antisocial behavior*, (pp. 318–355). Cambridge, UK: Cambridge University Press.

About the Author

After three decades in criminal justice, Jack Hobson retired as a police officer in 2011. He knew he wanted to be a police officer his whole life, but he was torn between his fascination with all things law enforcement and his love for reading and teaching. After graduating from college in Miami, Florida, Hobson joined a local police department south of Boston. He was quickly drawn to the education and training side of law enforcement, bringing community policing into the classroom. As his interest in proactive, prevention education grew, so did his interest in how children learn. To that end, he earned a Doctorate in Education.

Long before bullying became a tragically iconic buzz word, and long before school shootings rocked the consciousness of the nation, Hobson wanted to write a book about the drift theory of juvenile delinquency prevention—not as a textbook but as a series of essays about the kids within the school system and the schools he patrolled and protected. There, he worked hard to prevent problems before they happened. Dr. Hobson is now a Visiting Associate Professor in Criminal Justice in a large university south of Boston. His first book, *Drifters*, is the result.

CPSIA information can be obtained at www.ICGtesting.com
Printed in the USA
LVOW01s0451240114

370812LV00009B/82/P